Safety Net?

by Ryder Rogers

Authentic
LIFESTYLE

Copyright © 2002 Ryder Rogers
First published in 2002 by Authentic Lifestyle

08 07 06 05 04 03 02   7 6 5 4 3 2 1

Authentic Lifestyle is an imprint of Authentic Media,
PO Box 300, Carlisle, Cumbria, CA3 0QS, UK
PO Box 1047, Waynesboro, GA 30830-2047
www.paternoster-publishing.com

British Library Cataloguing in Publication Data

A catalogue record for this book is available from the British
Library
ISBN 1-85078-458-2

Cover design by FourNineZero
Printed in Great Britain by
Cox and Wyman, Reading, Berkshire

Contents

This book is dedicated to
the One
who loves and helps all us failures
and
to the memory of my parents
who taught me how to deal with failure
in a healthy way.

Foreword

I first met Ryder and Heather Rogers when they were planting a church in Bedfordshire, and they used to come over to our leaders' days in Chorleywood for some refreshment. Then to our surprise they left their church and family to become missionaries in Albania. After some years their time in Albania came to a sudden halt when all expatriots were told to leave because of the chaotic and dangerous situation in the country. Ryder has kept going through thick and thin, as this book clearly shows. Through a variety of painful experiences he has learned how to handle difficulties and, more importantly, how to handle failure. The wisdom he has gained he shares with us in this helpful book.

We live in a very success-orientated society. Failure seems unacceptable. Even Christians can be sucked into such a mindset, though the Bible is full of examples of failure that have been an important ingredient in the formation of the sort of person God can use.

Moses is a great example of this. Moses in his arrogance tried but failed in his attempt to rescue one of his fellow Jews and was forced to run away from Pharoah's wrath and ended up looking after sheep in the back side of the desert. However, what a life of luxury in Pharoah's courts had been unable to accomplish, the failure and the years in the wilderness achieved. Moses not only became the most humble man on the face of the earth, but also one of the greatest leaders of all time.

Ryder Rogers has written a book that bravely tackles the whole painful issue of failure. He explores the subject using many personal as well as biblical examples. 'This book,' he writes, 'is written to bring failure out of the closet and to give a safety net for those who are struggling to keep their balance on the tightrope of life.'

It is easy to be overwhelmed with painful feelings when one fails. An important part of the safety net will be having an understanding of how God can use failure. Another part will be learning how to handle failure when it occurs. Someone has said that failure does not mean you are a failure. We all experience failure at some point in our lives and to be able to keep our balance and not sink into depression or develop a failure syndrome is important. Winston Churchill once said that success was to move from one failure to another with enthusiasm. He was so right.

This book will help readers handle difficulty and failure in the right way and to gain wisdom and maturity in the process. I am sure it will help many who are struggling with seeming defeat in a success hungry society.

Mary Pytches

Introduction

'I can't take any more,' said the young mum, with blood dripping from her wrist, as I patiently tried to ease the razor blade from her other hand. 'I've had enough.'

A recent documentary about the UK revealed that suicide is the second highest cause of death among young people in Great Britain. One young, able, and attractive girl explained in that programme all about her feelings of constant unworthiness. Why did she feel so worthless? Simply because of the unrelenting pressure to succeed. 'There's no middle ground any more,' she said. 'It's success or failure.'

In the West we live in a 'performance'-orientated society, and in the rarefied atmosphere of success that this creates at times we are left gasping for air to breathe. These days everything is measured by achievement, and judged by the lack of it. Failure is the one damning word that people cannot cope with.

This book is written to bring failure out of the closet. It is written for those who are judged (or judge themselves) to be failures, for those who fear failure, and for those who want to know what it is like to fail. Its aim is to give a safety net to any who are struggling to keep their balance on the tightrope of life and especially to some who might be tempted to make a final jump of despair into oblivion.

I am also attempting to redress the balance, weighted towards fear and guilt, and to give another, more positive side to what is commonly judged as 'Failure'.

Only the other day, like a signpost to encourage me along this route, I was delighted to read a headline in *The Times* that grabbed my attention: *'Failure is nothing to Fear*, says Rowling'. The article described how, after receiving an honorary degree in literature at her Alma Mater, Exeter University, J.K. Rowling (of Harry Potter meteoric fame) gave a talk to an audience of graduating students. She admitted how much, as a student herself (who gained only a 2.2 degree in French and the Classics), she had been dogged by a fear of personal failure and taking risks. She went on to say that 'Almost all mistakes, apart from those involving a loaded gun, are beneficial in one way or another.' She concluded her speech with the hope that those who were graduating that day would not be 'constrained by a fear of failure'.

This book is about those of us who have fallen flat on our faces taking a wrong step, or who have crashed when trying to do something we've never done before. My plea is that it is time we lifted up our bloodied faces and said: 'I'm not a failure. Maybe I did do something that was wrong or went wrong, but at least I didn't just sit there and do nothing. I did something.'

One of Jesus' greatest condemnations was to the man who did nothing but bury everything in the ground. Why did he fail to do something? Maybe because he had failed before. Maybe because he couldn't trust others or even himself. He certainly felt insecure with his lord and master. Maybe he chose a hole in the ground for no other reason than the simple assumption that it was safer to bury what he had and not take any risks in life. Too many of us are like a puppy with a bone. We bury what we have or what we've done underground for another, and hopefully better, day . . . whenever that may be.

But buried things rarely stay just as they are. They have a tendency to decay. I got into trouble with a number of people in one of my churches when I preached about things in the past that had gone wrong and had been buried alive. Over the years, rather than dying off, those things had continued to fester, causing rotten or rigid relationships. 'Let's dig them up, kill them off, and give them a decent burial,' I pleaded.

Too often I hear people saying, 'Better to leave things be; don't go raking up the past', in the misguided assumption that things that are left alone will somehow disappear. 'Out of sight is out of mind', is what they think. But buried things don't die off quite so easily. They lie, like weeds below the surface, waiting to be disturbed or waiting for a better season to pop their heads up and eventually take over the garden of our lives.

Gardening is all the rage these days. Radical gardening, when the TV 'Ground Force' people do a 'make-over' to transform someone's old garden into something new. Yet often, before things get better, they get worse. In the course of events the hard-working team often have to get rid of a skip or two of rubbish or unwanted things. Generally the process is difficult, and patience and tempers are severely tried, but in the end, when it's all over, there is that smile of relief and delight as the owners look in amazement at the marvellous transformation.

In this book I'm attempting to dig up some of the fruitless patches in our lives, and root out some of our failures (plus a number of my own including one in particular that happened when my wife and I were evacuated from Albania when that country collapsed into anarchy). I want to look at them in the light of an incident in the Bible that over the years I have turned to, thought about, returned to, and spoken on, many times. It's a fisherman's tale of men who not only caught nothing after a night's fishing but also thought they had nothing to show after three years of following a friend who had just died. That story has stimulated me to think about issues like:

What is failure?
Why do we fail?
Are some people more prone to failure than others?
What do we do when we fail?
Is failure all that bad?
And what is the way out when we have made a mess of things?

These are some of the questions that in this book I will be attempting to 'walk through' on the sandy beach of Galilee, along with Jesus and seven of his runaway disciples.

So if you're ready to join the company, let's get going. . .

Chapter 1

A Safety Net?

'Who wants to be a Millionaire?' asked the blue and silver scratch card delivered with my beefburger and chips at the fast food shop. To succeed all I had to do was answer two questions correctly from the multiple choices the card offered me and then select a further box to see what I had won. Back at home with trembling finger I scratched away at my first answer. Correct. Then the second. Correct. Would I be a millionaire with my third selection? I scratched away at one of the final boxes with bated breath. 'You have won a free large Coke', the card revealed. Into the bin went the card.

What drives over half the nation to gamble away millions of pounds each week on the national lottery? It's the desire to win.

We all want to be winners of one kind or another. These days so many books in the High Street bookshops pander to this longing. Many of the titles on view are about the importance and benefits of success. 'How to Win in 5 EASY STEPS', 'Maximising your Potential', 'Self Realisation – the Way to Succeed'.

And Christian bookshops are not much different when they display titles like 'The Victorious Life', 'How to be an Overcomer', '101 Ways to Successful Soul Winning', 'How to succeed as a Christian', and so on. . . On one occasion some years ago I remember seeing a Bible called something like 'The *Victorious* Christian's

Bible'.

This, by way of being different, is a book about failure.

As a youngster I, like many others, was introduced to that required Sunday reading series of paperback books called 'Heroes'. More often than not they were given out as a Sunday School prize! Over the years I have read (and enjoyed) a number of biographical and autobiographical 'success' stories. But later, when I have given these glowing accounts a bit more thought and compared them to my own experience, well. . . Quite honestly most of them have usually ended up making me feel even more of a failure than I already think I am.

Of course, just about all of us desperately want to succeed. We are conditioned to it from an early age. Success means cuddles, sweets, praise, and later on more money, promotion and the easy life. Consequently, for most of us, the word 'FAILED' that appeared on school reports, examination result letters, driving test forms and job application replies, etc. have painful memories for us.

Thank God, I have some healthy memories of failure. There was the time when all my friends were promised a bike if they passed their 11+ (that was the state exam to get you to a Grammar School where, in those far off days, you took further exams to get you into university or a college). I had my own hopes of a bike too, despite the fact that my parents weren't that well off and so didn't promise me one. But mainly I just wanted to pass to go on to a better school.

What a trauma to hear from my buddies over the telephone that they had passed and were all going to the Grammar School and then to get my results plopping through the front door an hour or so later (due to the vagaries of the postman's round) informing me that I was going to the Secondary Mod., as I had failed. The salt in the wound was the way some of them turned up on my doorstep within minutes of the postman's arrival with spanking brand new bikes. Crestfallen, but putting on a brave face, I congratulated them, admired their bikes and thanked them for their offers that I could have a compensatory ride. What a day of hell I endured, as I continually had to explain shamefacedly that I had failed my 11+.

But then everything changed when Dad (who had gone to the Grammar School I was hoping to attend) came back from work that evening and told me to go into the garage to see something that was there. Leaning against the wall was a beautiful shining new bike!

'Why?' I stutteringly asked, unable to believe what I was seeing. 'I didn't pass the exam.'

'Son,' my father replied, 'We know that you did your best; we can't ask for more.'

From that moment on 'Failure' took on a new feel. Instead of being a rod to beat myself with, the feelings that accompanied failure became a walking stick to help me keep going along the uncertain and rocky path of life. What a difference a few positive words can make at the point of failure!

A decade or so later, after four years of hard work at Bible College studying for my Bachelor of Divinity degree, something similar and just as significant happened. Exam days had ended and a number of us 'students' were holidaying at a College Houseparty at the Keswick Convention (a two-week gathering for thousands of Christians in the Lake District for the deepening of one's spiritual life). For some masochistic reason our results were phoned through in the middle of the week and read out at the breakfast table. Those that had succeeded tried to look nonchalant when their results were intoned, while those who had failed tried to look appropriately 'Christianly content'. You can guess what was read after my name: 'FAILED'.

After congratulating my successful friends, I slipped off early to the Convention tent to sit there in the quiet and collect my rambling thoughts. The pianist came in early, and started to warm up. As he played, the words of the song that he was practising burned into my heart: 'I'd rather have Jesus than men's applause. I'd rather be faithful to his dear cause. I'd rather have Jesus than anything this world affords today.' It was as though this time my *heavenly* Father was saying to me, 'Son, I know you did your best.' And with that the peace of God breezed through my heart.

In failure encouragement is a healing ointment.

Conversely, like a burning and blasting wind that scores deep into our personality and leaves permanent

I'd put it on back to front . . . failed again.

scars, is the sort of verbal judgement we get when people say, as we attempt something difficult or new, 'You'll never do that. You can't succeed at anything.'

I was a novice to the Boys' Brigade (even though I was over thirty and pastoring my second church) and, as chaplain, officially second-in-command to the Company. As I looked at all those orderly eager ranks of boys on parade, I secretly panicked at their efficiency and my ignorance. My induction as chaplain at the Annual Display was no encouragement to me either! Before the Annual Display I was carefully shown how to remove my Glengarry, flicking the tabs inside in order to place it on my left shoulder for the National Anthem. All went well until I replaced the thing on my head in order to salute the flag. As I did so the tabs slipped down – over my face! I'd put the cap on back to front. Failed again!

I suppose, as a result, I had sympathy with those lads who also made mistakes and didn't come up to scratch. One lad in the Company tried so hard to do things right, but always something was wrong. His hat wasn't on correctly (two fingers above the eyebrow), his tie a bit askew, his belt not shiny enough, a bit of mud was splattered on his trousers or shoes as he ran down to church to get there on time (or as near 'on time' as possible). Whenever, in Drill Practice, the command was given to 'Left turn', he invariably turned right and vice versa. Again I could sympathise with the lad as I had the same sort of problems with left and right. That was until I was about thirty-five years old and a helpful doctor told me his secret.

'Hold your hand in front of you, palm away from you, thumb pointing horizontally and at right-angles to the other fingers,' he told me. 'If there is an L-shape between fingers and thumb it's your "L"eft hand, if not it's your right.'

And it worked. Even today, at the ripe old age of fifty-seven, as I talk I wave a hand in front of my face to see if there is an 'L' in front of me and then I confidently say, 'Yes. It's on the left.'

Back to our problematical young BB boy. Whenever the order was barked 'Halt' and the combined feet of the squad clattered together to a unified halt you always knew who (like Jones in Dad's Army) had created the solitary echoing last footstep.

Once, when he made yet another slow response, he was asked by an exasperated officer, 'What are you thinking about? What's fluttering around inside that brain of yours? Butterflies?'

'You'll never get anywhere in life,' he was told firmly in front of all the other grinning boys.

Typical failure material in their estimation.

I had the privilege of counselling that same young lad on a couple of occasions. Once when I had the joy of helping him to trust the Lord Jesus as his Saviour, and the next time (sadly after he had left our church, but still kept in touch with me as a neighbour and friend) to pray with him about the judgements made against him throughout his life. At the end of this second time of prayer I felt it was right to encourage him to go with the sense he had that God was calling him to serve him full-time in evangelism.

Never do anything?!

That 'butterfly-brained' lad was consequently accepted to serve on Ship Logos with Operation Mobilisation, later went to an understanding and supportive Bible College, joined an international evangelistic association, travelled the world, led literally thousands to the Lord, and now has begun his own evangelistic organisation in the Far East. What might, or might not, have happened if he had believed those earlier judgements on his abilities, or apparent lack of them?

Worst of all, however, is the statement that thought-less people make when they say, 'You're a failure.' That is something that belittles not just our abilities but our very being and can be almost like a curse on us.

There are people who have lived all their lives under a cloud of inadequacy and failure because as unplanned and unwanted children they were told, 'You were a mistake'. Having been judged mistakes, they made mistakes. Failure is as failure's told.

What we are dubbed, we often do. When I began teaching at a secondary modern school in Essex, for some reason one class of troublemakers dubbed me with the nickname 'Hitler'. My wife said it was because of my little moustache, but that didn't look anything like Hitler's! Maybe it was the way I clicked down the corridor with metal Blakey studs (great money savers for poor ex-students just married) on the heels of my shoes. Whatever it was, after a few weary weeks of behind-the-back, behind-the-hand comments, I got the class together and warned them: 'Call me Hitler enough, Hitler I'll become.' That stopped them.

What we are called we often become.

Was that why, when Jesus was talking to the twelve on a hillside one day, he said, 'Don't call anyone an idiot or a moron'? Those who make mistakes are conditioned to feel inadequate and insecure and as a result do more things wrong. And all the more so if they are called failures. Say something often enough and people will believe you.

Try an experiment that shows how powerful the mind is. Tell another person in a warm car or room that they are tired and going to yawn. Describe the stretchy feeling at the back of the throat. Ask them if they can feel it beginning. Tell them that it's coming. Their tongue is pulling down and back. Then draw in a lovely slow juddering breath. And watch them yawn. Or get someone to walk along a narrow piece of wood, like a sea breakwater (preferably with water on both sides) without looking down, and keep on saying to them at each step, 'Watch it. Mind. You're going to fall.' Sooner or later they'll lose their nerve and either stop or fall off and into the water.

What we are told enough, we do. And what we do, we think we are.

Another problem that this word 'failure' creates (because failure in our 'success-orientated' culture is socially unacceptable) is the tendency to cover up our failure in order to appear more successful and acceptable to others. The whole of the Beauty Business has built itself on 'image'. The idea that this product or that will either cure or cover up our blemishes so that we will become the most beautiful and desirable creature on God's earth – is most appealing! Consequently when we fail, because of our perceived 'image', we panic in case people find the real us. We look for a cosmetic cover-up. Most times we then go on to build a more permanent little shell around us, which over time can become quite a big and tough one. Inside we are ashamed of who we are, so we do one of two things. Either we withdraw into the hard unyielding shell of fear or we become brazenly aggressive in order to compensate. Sometimes we even manage to fool ourselves that we have, after all, succeeded (when really we haven't), and so we live our lives under a delusion or a lie.

But is failure necessarily all that bad? Is failure really such a negative thing? I suppose it all depends on how we define failure, what it is and how we treat it. There is a verse of the Bible that has often intrigued me. It's really a comment on how we look at and handle failure. Paul wrote to a church that was at the centre of the morally crumbling empire of his day about how every man, woman and child has a little voice inside called conscience that 'accuses or excuses them'. But then he goes on to say how so often when this God-given conscience works we humans abuse and misuse it.

I've been saddened, over many years of listening to Christian people as they talk about their problems, to discover how they do one or the other of those two things – but generally the wrong way round. At times I've been gob-smacked to hear some of them go to such lengths to *excuse* themselves for the things that God would unquestioningly call a moral failure. In fact it's all a matter of excuses, excuses, excuses.

At other times, and at the opposite end of the spectrum, there are those sensitive souls who continually rake over the past for things that they have done, or not done, and *accuse* themselves to such an extent that they make themselves feel the world's most terrible failures. When we get to the bottom of things usually I find that the things they dredge up are issues that in God's loving eyes were forgiven years ago.

And society does something similar when it constantly and consistently makes excuses for those things that are clearly against God and what he says (*excusing* moral failure as merely a personal matter) while at the same time *accusing* the church of narrow-mindedness and dogmatism because it has the audacity to speak out (accusing the church of political incorrectness). Society, despite defending the democratic right of the individual, doesn't like it when people are non-conformist and refuse to tow the line of popular opinion.

And, in general, people in the West today are more concerned with their material standard of living than they are with issues of moral integrity. We, are permissive of infidelity and falsehood in government so long as the economy is doing well. The argument that the world makes is, 'Why rock the boat when the money in your pocket is so strong?'

And that's the bottom line. Pragmatism and profit,

not principals.

What double standards we practise. Touching someone else's wife is okay, but touch mine . . . !

God gives us another way.

King David, many thousand years ago, was in the same leaky boat of moral failure (and the pound in the peoples' pockets wasn't doing so badly then either), but a brave prophet pointed out his wrongs to him. David was then humble enough to admit his faults and publically stated there was no distinction between social and spiritual failure. He said about his deceitful, adulterous affair and bloody cover-up, 'What I did was against God as well as people.'

Jesus took the same sort of line in his story of the tearaway son who lived in the fast lane and lost all his father's hard-earned money. The crunch in the story comes when the boy admits to himself, and then to his father, 'Dad, I'm sorry. I've done wrong to both you and God.' What we do privately or publicly affects both God and us – there are no distinctions.

Failure fractures us, our relationship with God, and society, and can ultimately be fatal.

Since working in Albania for these past eight years I have never flown so many thousands of miles. But I have to admit that every time we take off I still have a sneaking feeling that God never intended us to be up there so near to his home. A failed aircraft engine these days is usually a disaster to all who are flying in the plane, despite the stewardess's cheerful face as she shows the passengers how to put on their oxygen masks and find their life-jacket under the seat as the aircraft taxis off.

Yet as we lift off into the sky in yet another 747 I remember how many times the Wright brothers crashed before they finally achieved their first recognised prolonged flight. For them failure was part of the learning curve. How many filaments burned through, and how many glass bowls shattered, before Edison discovered his final and successful incandescent light bulb? How many engines blew up before Stephenson perfected his Rocket?

Most of life's advances are surrounded by the litter of failure. The one who said, 'If at first you don't succeed try, try again', was a source of great wisdom. Failure is not necessarily the end of things that it so often appears or is said to be. In fact, the very attempting of a thing, though the result may seem to be a failure, is a form of success. A friend of mine was fond of saying, 'Better to have failed, than to have done nothing.' And another used to say, 'Better to do a job badly than not to do anything.' Or as Shakespeare, the famous bard put it, 'Better to have loved and lost than never to have loved at all.'

At least failure means that something has been tried.

At my secondary school (following my 11+ fiasco) I was considered a failure at woodwork. After two years of carpentry classes the only thing that I managed to produce, which the Woodwork master said might be considered good enough to take home as a present for my Mum, was a wooden tray. (Believe it or not it is still useable more than forty years later!) Generally in my report he said something like, 'Enthusiastic but lacking ability.' Twenty years later I built a kennel for our dog that was more like a fortress. It was so heavy that it could hardly be lifted, probably due to all the screws used as nails to hold it together!

Nine years after this 'success' my wife and I, and a church family that we had formed, started to build a church building all on our own. When I told my mother what we were doing she looked sideways at the tray and then to add salt into the wound she jokingly added, 'You could hardly build a kennel.' But I did it. I built both a kennel and a church.

During my school days in our English Literature classes we had to study and learn by heart different poems. I remember the one by Rudyard Kipling that began 'IF . . .' and the line, 'If you can meet with triumph and disaster and treat those two imposters just the same . . . you'll be a man my son.'

The disaster of failure can often be an imposter because it is based on the judgements and norms of others.

And there are many people who are impossible to please – like the person who says, 'Anyone who is less enthusiastic than me is lazy, more enthusiastic than me a fanatic, and believes differently from me is a heretic.'

So, where, I wonder, is that nebulous line drawn that marks out success from failure? On one of our brief visits to the UK from the busy work we were doing in Albania I had the joy of seeing our grandson lurch from the supporting arms of his mother into the welcoming arms of his grandmother as he took his first three stumbling, uncoordinated, steps all mixed up together.

Success or failure?

For him it was success. For me it would be considered a pathetic failure. People would say that I was drunk if that was all I could do. But then, on the other hand, if I were to have a paralysing stroke that left me bed-ridden, and one day I got out of bed and managed to stumble three steps before collapsing into an armchair, that would be a great success.

Circumstances alter cases. We can easily get confused, by comparing the failure of one person with the success of another (or even our own one-time success with our present failure), and so make a false judgement about it all.

Two questions come to mind.

First. What is in our heart at the time of our so-called

Chapter 2

Setting the Scene

It was the fourth Easter in Albania that we had spent in the village where we had gone to live and work. Cornflakes (a recently imported luxury), hot fresh bread just collected from the baker's wood-fired oven round the corner, home-made marmalade and a slice of the Bible to set us up for the day, was how it all started. We had just read about the disciples having their own breakfast on the beach with Jesus a couple of weeks after his resurrection. The ensuing discussion between my wife and I during our daily prayer-time set my mind off on a journey down the road we call 'Failure'.

Maybe at this point a free translation would help to set the scene for our journey together.

But hold it a minute. If you are anything like me, when you see a quote from the Bible, you tend to say, 'I know that bit', and so skip reading it. I must admit that I really have to discipline myself to read any Bible passages that are printed in a book. But when I do make the effort I often come across something new to think about. So, read with me what may be a familiar story that, hopefully, is put in a fresh way.

John's description of a special day or
John sets the record straight

Once more, after what seemed to be a long period of waiting, Jesus showed himself to be alive to some of his followers, this time by the Sea of Galilee.

It happened like this:

Simon (also given the name Peter), Thomas (nicknamed the Twin), Nathaniel (from a village in the Galilee region called Cana), the two sons of Zebedee (James and John), and two other followers of Jesus were all gathered together.

Simon Peter said to them all, 'I don't know about you, but I'm off fishing.'

They said, 'Great, we'll come with you.'

So as a group they went back to Galilee, found one of their old boats and got into it. But despite fishing all night they didn't catch a single thing.

Early the next day, as the morning light flecked across the grey dawn sky, Jesus stood on the beach, but none of his friends recognised him.

Seeing how high out of the water the boat was riding, he called out to them: 'Hello there my friends, it doesn't look as though you have caught anything.'

'No,' they replied curtly.

'Why don't you throw your nets over on the right side of the boat. Do it now and you'll find something there,' Jesus promised them.

When they did the thing he told them they now found that they weren't able to get the net back into the boat because it was so full of fish – a whole shoal of them.

At this point the disciple who knew more than any of the others that Jesus loved him said to Peter, 'You know who it is – it's the Lord.'

As soon as Simon Peter heard him say that it was the Lord, he grabbed his clothes and flung them on (as he was stripped

*off for work) and without thinking threw himself into the
water. Fortunately they were less than a hundred metres from
the beach.*

*The other men followed Peter to shore in the boat, dragging
behind them the net that was full of fish.*

*When they touched land the first thing they saw was a
charcoal fire burning, some fish cooking on it, and to one side
some fresh bread.*

*Jesus told them, 'Bring me some of the fish that you have
just caught.'*

*Simon Peter rushed back, clambered into the boat, grabbed
the net, and dragged it up onto the beach with the whole catch
of 153 large fish. It was amazing that with so many fish in it
the net hadn't split.*

*Jesus gave them all an invitation. 'Come and share break-
fast with me.'*

*Not one of Jesus's followers dared ask, 'Who are you?'
because they didn't need anyone to tell them, they all simply
just* knew *– it was Jesus their Lord.*

*Jesus went over and took the bread and gave it to them, bit by
bit, one by one. And he did the same with the fish he'd prepared.*

*This was the third time that Jesus had visibly appeared and
showed himself to them all, proving that he really was alive
after being buried in the grave.*

*When they had eaten enough food Jesus turned directly to
Simon Peter and asked, 'Simon, son of John, do you remember
saying that you loved me more than anyone and anything
else? Is that still the case?'*

*'Yes, Lord,' he replied a little apprehensively, 'You know
that you are very special to me.'*

*'Well then,' Jesus continued, 'those who follow me like
young lambs, you must share with them the things that will
make them strong.'*

*A bit later Jesus asked again, 'Simon, son of John, do you
really love me?'*

Peter answered as last time but more emphatically, 'Yes, Lord, you know how much I care for you.'

'Then look after the older ones in my flock, as well as the young.'

For a third time Jesus asked Peter the same direct and unsettling question, 'Simon, son of John, is it true that you really do care for me?'

Peter was upset because Jesus for the third time questioned him about whether, and how much, he cared for him, so he said, 'Lord, you know everything about me, you know what my feelings are for you.'

Jesus said, 'Be a shepherd to my sheep and provide for them.'

Then he continued. 'Now listen while I tell you something that's a fact. When you were a youngster you dressed yourself and went off where you wanted, but when you are old you will have to hold out your hands for someone else to dress you and then they will take you where you don't want to go.'

Now . . . are you ready to follow me?

In a subtle way Jesus was actually foretelling the sort of death that Peter would have to go through. Though in fact that death would be for the glory and praise of God.

Finally Jesus said, 'Now ask yourself in the light of this, are you ready to follow me?'

At that point Peter looked around and saw that John, the disciple who seemed to have a special friendship with Jesus, was approaching.

John was the one who at their last supper together, which was a Passover meal, sat next to Jesus with his arm round his shoulder and had quietly asked him, 'Lord, who is this person who would dare to betray you?'

When Peter saw John approaching them on the beach he quickly and deftly turned the conversation by asking Jesus, 'But Lord, what about him?'

Jesus replied, 'If I want him to stay alive until I come back again at the end of the world, what's that got to do with you? What you *must do is forget about others and make sure you are following me.'*

On the basis of this comment, an unfounded rumour started and spread in the family of the church that John wouldn't ever have to die.

But in fact, to put the record straight, Jesus didn't say that. What he did say was, 'If I want him to stay alive until I come back again at the end of the world what's that got to do with you, Peter?'

I should know, because I'm the one who was there, who heard all this. I made a note of what Jesus said because we know that whatever Jesus says is sure to happen.

#This account can be found in John's Gospel chapter 21 and verses 1 to 24.

On the morning that we read this piece of the Bible together, Heather, my wife, said something about Peter's feelings of insecurity and how he deflected Jesus' attention to John. To which I replied, 'Well, we all want a safety net!'

As I went through the day I chewed over in my mind the story of this third resurrection appearance. I couldn't get away from the idea of safety nets.

Thoughts began to form and develop in my little brain about this fundamental issue of failure and the ways we cope with it. Throughout life we consciously or unconsciously set up safety nets – sort of 'fall-back' mechanisms – just in case. And if we haven't done that when things go wrong we quickly look for a net of some kind to fall into. It can be something or someone, a defence action or attitude, but we soon make sure that we've got a safety net firmly and securely installed. Because if we don't the results can be disastrous.

This book is basically the result of a personal journey and meditation on that section from John's personal account of events. It meanders around the theme of 'Failure' and our need for a 'Safety Net'.

Chapter 3

The Need for a Net – For Our Sakes

We were camping with our family near York and had taken the children to see the more historic parts of the city. Unfortunately (for me) they wanted to walk along some of the ancient walls. Unfortunately for me, I say, as I haven't got a head for heights. This was something my wife, who loved climbing mountains, discovered about me as a new bride.

In the first year of our marriage we went camping and pitched our tent for a few days near to Glastonbury. One day we went into Glastonbury to walk up the Tor. Halfway up, aware that I wasn't at her side, she looked back and to her surprise saw me rigidly spread-eagled against the bank at the side of the path that was taking us to the top. For a number of minutes, paralysed with fear because of the drop at the other side of the path, I stood there with my eyes closed, unable to move either up or down.

Over the years I had tried to overcome my fears. So, many years later, having become the father of two young daughters, and determined not to spoil the children's fun I agreed to walk along the walls of York with them.

Things weren't too bad at the beginning as I was able to avoid getting too close to any edges. But after a while what I dreaded happened – we came to a narrow bit with a drop away at the side.

The tension started in my calves and shot with a tingle up to, and through, my spine.

Helplessly I called for my eldest daughter, who was twelve at the time, to look after me. She proudly took my hand, while I meekly followed her like a lamb.

'Wasn't it a lovely view from the walls?' I was asked when it was all over.

'I don't know,' I admitted, 'I had my eyes shut.'

There was nothing wrong with the view, nothing wrong with the walls, nothing wrong with the journey that thousands make every year. The problem was me. I need something big and solid between me and any drop of more than ten feet, or I sweat, sway, and am ready to slip. That barrier, whatever it may be, is necessary for me as my safety net.

I know when and how my problem began. We were in Wales for a holiday – Mum and Dad and me. I was about seven at the time. We had chugged up some mountain or other in my father's old Morris, and at the top had stopped to look at the scenery. For some reason my parents had got out to see the view before me. I ran to join them at the place where they stood at the side of the road. As I approached them and the precipitous drop to look at the scene a thousand or so feet directly below us, suddenly the edge of the mountain seemed to evaporate before me and I felt I was gradually toppling over the edge. My world went spinning into helpless chaos as my parents grabbed their white-faced little pride and joy before he fainted and fell into the abyss below.

Ever since that day a feeling of weakness in my legs and a sensation of beginning to float in space buzzes through my head as surges of electrical tension course up and down my body.

Every July we, as a family, spent a week camped on the Scripture Union site at the foot of Skiddaw for the Keswick Convention. Every year I had to let my wife and my two girls leave me half way up the mountain on our annual pilgrimage so that they could press on to higher ground towards the top without me. And every year I felt a sense of failure – especially when my youngest daughter, who was only five years old at the time, made it all the way to the summit!

How I hated those feelings that defeated me in my desire to 'reach the heights' – though you wouldn't have thought so many years later if you had seen me climbing on all fours up the roof of the church we were building and sitting on the ridge tiles so as to sort out the lead flashing! The ability to run up the roof took months (even years) of steady acclimatisation and gaining a bit more height each week.

Then, sadly, without the familiarity of the heights I had gained, the fears returned. Maybe the problem is worse now because I know I *have* done it, but at this present moment, once again, I can't scramble onto any roof or anything too high. Even a tallish ladder defeats me. The old familiar feelings of dizziness rush in, unsought and unwanted.

Many of us need safety nets for our own unsteady emotion's sake. Emotions are good friends but poor masters. They're great when they function well and properly. They can identify and express what's going on inside, even acting as a safety valve. But emotions can also create havoc when they malfunction and operate in an unhealthy or unreal way, especially when they get out of hand and take over.

As I thought long and hard on the *feelings* of those close friends of Jesus I marvelled at the rollercoaster of emotions that they must have gone through.

One of the hardest emotions that people have to go through is that of feeling forsaken – whether that feeling is caused by a broken relationship, divorce, bereavement after a happy marriage, or sudden redundancy. Close relationships when they get shaken or smashed give way to loneliness, despair and the cry for some greater security.

Peter and the Galilee Gang had been close friends with Jesus for three years. Maybe that doesn't seem long until you realise what those three years involved. For them it was three years, day after day, hour after hour, of walking, talking, eating, watching, sharing, questioning and being questioned, hearing, helping, laughing, crying, singing, praying, learning and following as they travelled hundreds of dusty miles together circling Palestine.

Such a deep friendship had been struck that they felt that there were no secrets between them. Jesus had somehow plumbed the depths of their being, dredged up the dirt, cleaned off all the scum that rose to the surface, filled them with a new sense of value that they had never known before, and had shown them the meaning of honest and open relationships. Friendship meant that he, as their master, could at one moment commend them, the next rebuke them, and then paradoxically get down on his hands and knees and wash their feet.

One of the things that is so different here in Albania is to see men walking down the road arm in arm, or hand in hand. In my early days here, with my British reserve, I found that I was a bit unsettled by that. If men holding hands and carrying a flower seems a bit unmasculine, then visualise them with a couple Kalashnikovs carelessly slung over their shoulders and a few grenades strapped round their waists. That's how we were going to see many of them during and after the State of Emergency. A memory like that soon blows away any sense of unmanliness, and they would blow you away if you were to question any of them about their manhood.

So now that I've been living in a culture like that for a while I have no problem with seeing in my mind Jesus and Peter with their arms round one another discussing the kingdom of God together. Neither do I have difficulty in visualising John at the disciples' Last Supper before Jesus went to the cross, with his head on Jesus' shoulder. John talks openly about his friendship with Jesus, leading up to their last meal together, in normal Eastern   cultural terms. He also records Jesus' question to Peter, which for us in the West is somewhat embarrassing, 'Simon, son of John, how do you *feel* about me? Do you *love* me?' Again with my old British mind-set I react inwardly with a 'Yuk'. But with my Albanian cultural hat on I quite understand people who are not afraid of talking about, nor embarrassed to show, their emotions.

You ought to visit our neighbours here when someone has just died, as they sit around the body rocking with grief, sobbing, and singing out their feelings. And later you should join the family and those who live nearby as they pass the coffin from one to another down the road. Hear the grief-stricken children, as they carry their paper wreaths, gasping between their tears, 'O father, O daddy of mine. I want my dadda. Come back O my father.' See with us the women being virtually carried down the road as they shriek out their grief. It is then that you start to get into a more biblical mind-set.

We have learned over the years that to invest in close friendship pays high dividends, but it is a costly thing because it involves love – and love feels not only joy and closeness, but sorrow and separation.

The painful truth is, after a really close relationship when you are left alone, it hurts.

My Mum suffered from rejection as a child. Her mother (my grandmother) had endured fifteen younger brothers and sisters. She had to be a mother to all fifteen of them while her own mother was producing the next offspring. So my mother's mother had very distinct and very negative views about children and sex and often said to my mother, 'We never wanted you.'

After hearing and suffering so often from these negative comments throughout her childhood and youth, and then to be loved unconditionally by a handsome, caring, strong, gentle young man (my father), that was the fulfilment of all she could have ever longed for. Sadly, because of her damaged self-image she felt unworthy of his love or anyone else's. This was something a number of her early letters to him revealed – letters we discovered many years after her death.

Sadly, in his forties he was struck down and hospitalised with a serious heart condition, operated on by Britain's first heart transplant team, but died unexpectedly a few years later. All this was a devastating tragedy for her. As he became dangerously ill, the realisation of losing the one who had loved her unconditionally brought on a severe nervous breakdown. And when he died later at just fifty-one years of age it plunged her back into the depths. Death for her meant not only fractured friendship but feelings of devastating forsakeness.

'Oh, to have someone to talk to at nights – to share the little things that have happened – and to have someone to cuddle,' was her plaintive longing and cry.

I remember a widow I visited in one of my churches who daily bemoaned her husband's death some twenty years earlier by saying, 'You can live too close.'

It is not just the bereaved, but the divorced also, who feel in need of a safety net. Divorce is just as traumatic as bereavement, despite the trite comment some thought-less people make that there are many more pebbles on the beach. Divorce leaves divorcees with raw emotions of anger and guilt. It makes them feel desperately vul-nerable. However, unlike the bereaved, there is no real closure. Oh yes, there may be a piece of legal paperwork that says the marriage is dead, but unfortunately the corpse can still be unexpectedly met when out shopping, queuing for a show, or worshipping at an inter-church celebration.

Where does a divorced person turn to when wanting to share some feeling – good or bad? Who really wants to listen to the humdrum things that have happened to you during the day? Who will take the screaming kids off your hands for a day of peace and quiet? What do you do if you don't know how to fix the central heating system and the income is halved or reduced to merely an assistance grant? Who can you ever trust to get close to you again? Where was God in all of the struggles, and where is he now?

Where is the net when friendship fails?

The disciples felt forsaken in their bereavement, in the divorce of death. They felt alone – even in their own frightened crowd. What now, apart from locking them-selves up in a secret room?

Then the disciples felt *confused*. Life had been so cer-tain. It had been in vivid colours when Jesus was with them. He knew the way, he told them where they were going, what they were about to do, what God had on his agenda for them. Now life was all a monochrome of uncertainty. Confusion weaved its sticky web around their hearts, minds and feet. It was paralysing – like the panic that crept up and around me on Glastonbury Tor.

In the same way, sudden debilitating sickness, unemployment, or so called 'early retirement' brings confusion. It takes away life's certainties. Everything becomes questionable as the lights go out on life as we know it.

Again imagine how it was for these seven disciples. For three years they had been tazzing breathlessly around Palestine, up north, down south, across the middle and back again. Life was non-stop, at times without a moment's peace and quiet, and sometimes even without space to sit down and eat a hurried meal. They were busy preparing the way for Jesus in cities and villages, preaching about the need for repentance, healing the sick, casting out demons, seeing Jesus was safely protected from the over-imposing crowds and all those doting parents with their pesky children, sorting out transport (boats and donkeys, etc.), arranging hospitality and finally finding a room for a last supper. Phew!

Then it all came to a standstill.

Suddenly their world came crashing down around their ears to a final, frightening and confusing full stop.

The secretary of my first church during the service to welcome me as pastor into my second church warned the members what I was like. 'This young man,' he said, pointing to me, 'keeps going and is difficult to stop. What you need to do is find his ignition key and switch him off.'

But God knew where the key was and one day *he* switched me off. For five years I had rushed around preaching, visiting the sick and elderly, evangelising, sorting out peoples' problems, getting involved with the young people, training Sunday School teachers, etc., etc. Then one summer Sunday night after an open air service on the quayside of Brixham harbour I just about managed to struggle back to my home feeling physically sick, with a pounding head and struggling with a spine that seemed to be falling apart at every step.

Next day I was rushed by ambulance into the isolation ward of Torbay hospital with meningitis, forbidden to see my daughters and to kiss my wife who now had to wear a face mask every time she visited me.

For three months I could do nothing. It took another three more months just to learn to ease back into being a husband and father again, and yet another three months to slowly start to pick up responsibilities in the church.

For nine months, non-stop, my head throbbed and ached.

It was hard being suddenly halted in my tracks and having to learn that I was not indispensable.

When all that we are accustomed to comes to an abrupt stop – what then?

Often after the whirlwind of 'activities' has stormed in and out of our lives – rushing through and leaving a broken door of exhaustion swinging at an odd angle on its buckled hinges – there then subtly creeps in through the unprotected opening all sorts of uncertainties and confusion.

It must have been a bit like that for these followers of Jesus. All that the disciples had gradually come to be certain of was blown away on that fateful Friday that we now call Good Friday. Interesting isn't it how that Friday of seeming failure eventually got to be called Good Friday! For them it was anything but good. It was Bloody Black Friday.

The abnormal, supernatural darkness that lasted from midday to three o'clock in the afternoon on that terrible and traumatic day seemed to reflect their own feelings and experience. For them it was the darkness of not seeing rhyme nor reason. It was that black impenetrable gloom that has no answer to the question 'Why?' It was the darkness of not knowing what was going on. It was the darkness of confusion, of no longer understanding anything any more. Nothing made sense any longer.

For me the comment of the two on the road to the village of Emmaus seems to sum up all the accumulated feelings and frustrations of those disappointed disciples. 'We thought and hoped that he was the one who was going to save Israel, but now. . .' The certainties that they had gradually found in Jesus had crumbled just at the time they were needed. The safety net was gone. So what now? All the successes that had been achieved over the years, what did they count for at this black and desolate moment? Everything had gone to pot. The thought of failure – theirs as well as Jesus' – hedged them in at every turn.

Oh yes, failed hopes intermingled with failed lives make a potent poison.

Judas was a man of high hopes. He believed that Jesus would change the face of politics in Israel by bringing in God's kingdom of power. That divinely ordained kingdom, he believed, would overcome and expel the Romans and set up the nation of Israel. They, the chosen ones, would do the seeming impossible with a renewed spiritual fervour that would put Judaism back on its historic foundation of divine favour. But Jesus appeared to have a different agenda, more to do with love than revolution, humility than power. And the final embarrassment was his arrival at the capital on a donkey – even though that was something that Zechariah had said would happen some five centuries beforehand!

Judas's hopes ended up in the dust, just like all the coats that he saw under the donkey's hooves. He thought that people should have been waving swords not branches!

So, at their last Passover meal together, when Jesus, maybe as a last-ditch effort to break down Judas's defences, handed over to him the 'love portion' – the last bit of bread that wiped the meat bowl clean, generally given to the favourite child – Judas's shortsighted eyes were still focused on the dust and broken branches (a bit like how he saw only a puddle of wasted money after Mary had anointed Jesus with costly oil). At that point of the meal we're told the devil took control of the handle of disappointment in the heart of Judas and drove him into the night.

Driven by demons, disillusionment and despair, especially after Jesus failed to resist his arrest and was finally condemned to be killed on the cross, Judas did away with himself on the end of a length of rope that gave way, like his hopes, spilling his disillusioned guts all over the place.

This is the Judas Syndrome. Beware.

At the same time how confused and unsettled the remaining eleven must have all felt. The sight and smell of torches in the night shook them out of their sleepy state in that peaceful garden of prayer. A sharp ring of steel echoed among the sighings of the sleepy olive branches that like a stirred conscience whispered 'Cowards' as they all ran off into the dark security of the night. They scattered like frightened sheep on the hillside, just as Jesus had forewarned, as they left him to face his fate alone.

Peter more than most must have been swamped with overwhelming feelings of guilt. He'd betrayed his friend. Despite a token swing of his sword in the darkness of the shadowy garden, later, in the flickering light of the fires around the High Priest's courtyard, he'd lied, denied, and cursed with fright at the very mention of the name of Jesus. No wonder he left in tears.

I sympathise with Peter's feelings of failure. We had been in Albania for just over three years when the country started to fall apart. People throughout the country had invested in financial pyramid schemes which had gone bankrupt. The Government didn't seem to be interested in helping, and rumours went around that ministers and officials were getting their own percentages. Down in the south students and workers went on strike. The Government declared a State of Emergency, banning public meetings, enforcing a curfew, silencing the BBC and Voice of America as people started to riot.

Suddenly everyone was taking up arms. Army depots were broken into, guards were shot, anarchy broke out and swept like a tidal wave up from the south right to the administrative region of the capital city, Tirana. The north, which supported the President, reacted and also took up arms, and gunfire was heard in increasing intensity and proximity in our village.

On its shortwave World Service the BBC began to advise all British citizens to leave Albania. Foreigners were leaving in their hordes. The planes and ferries were filled with anxious businessmen and families eager to get out of this collapsing state.

What were we to do as the only foreigners in our village some five miles north of the capital?

Well, we had prayed about it over the past week and felt that we should stay put. So when neighbours anxiously asked, 'Are you afraid?' we honestly replied, 'No.' To prove it, on the evening when the local arms depot was broken into and tracer bullets all night lit the blackened sky (the electricity had been cut by someone), and despite Kalashnikovs and automatic gunfire that reverberated through the night hours both sides of our house and less than six feet from our bedroom window, I, so my wife tells me, slept like a baby.

'Are you going to leave us?' our friends asked as we surfaced the next morning to chat outside our high walled gardens and watch the children picking up empty cartridges and used shells. 'No,' we answered as we went off down the road to catch the local bus to go into the capital for our regular Thursday language lesson.

Along the side of the roads the police check-points that had dotted all routes in and out of the capital had disappeared overnight. In their place gangs of youths with machine guns gathered at different places along the main road, the route that our bus was taking.

Our language teacher, who arrived late, was too distraught to give us a lesson, and anyway we were the only foreigners who wanted one.

After a while of chatting with people at our mission centre we then went off to see how our neighbour's daughter had got on after a small operation on her hand. While we were looking for her at the clinic set up by the missionary community, a message came through on the telephone. 'If Ryder and Heather are there tell them to come immediately to the Baptist Centre.' So off we toddled.

When we got there computers were being packed up and other valuable equipment was being sorted out for storage. On entering the busy office we were told, 'You have two hours to return to your village with a centre vehicle, and pack a shoulder bag each. When you return we will all be going to the British Embassy for an evacuation.'

'But we're not leaving,' we stated with seraphic smiles.

'You are!' we were forcefully informed. 'Our missionary society says so on the advice of the Foreign Office and British Embassy.'

'But we were given freedom by the regional director to make our own on-the-ground decision,' we replied.

'There is to be no discussion about it. We are *all* to leave.'

So off we went in the white Land Rover they gave us, in a state of confusion and shock. Our driver, Hajradini, sped along the main roads that were miraculously emptying of vehicles but steadily filling with looters who were using bicycles and wheelbarrows to carry off stolen bags of flour from the main flour depots on the way. 'Shumë keq (very bad),' he muttered under his breath as we travelled back to our village.

When we got to our village of Bregu-i-Lumit we sent out messengers to call together the church that we over the years had formed in our home. I fetched a couple on the back of my moped.

With tears we told them of the orders given by the British Foreign Office (that were being repeated every half hour on our shortwave radio), our Embassy and Society. We sorted out who would take on what responsibilities in the church, gave the musical instruments to the members of the worship group for safe keeping and to use at the Sunday services. With trembling voice I read to them Paul's farewell speech to the Ephesian Church from Acts 20 (that warns new Christians about the need to be faithful to the Lord whatever), and then prayed with them. We hurriedly hugged and kissed them all, then grabbed our passports and shoulder bag of essentials (how few things a person *really* needs at such times) jumped into the Land Rover that Dini was revving up, not having time to say goodbye to our dog, and with blurred vision waved goodbye to the tearful crowd of neighbours and friends who had gathered to say 'God bless you and keep you.'

It was just like a dream, or worse than that, more like a nightmare.

Then there was the gathering of the Brits at the Embassy; hearing that one of our colleagues had been shot in the head at the port to which we would be soon going; starting off in a convoy that got split up; being stopped and threatened by a gang of youths with iron bars who fiercely demanded our valuables above the echo of constant gunfire; the groups of armed men suspiciously eyeing us on the way; arriving at the sea port of Durres where people were burning down the custom's offices and smashing down doors into the warehouses; waiting by the cranes in a deserted part of

It was just like a dream, or worse than that, more like a nightmare.

the harbour only to see our rescue helicopters turn back; having to move to another quayside in the shadow of an oil storage tank as tracer bullets whined over head; being shot at by Italian sailors with machine guns and stun grenades; being abandoned after the Italian Navy took away only their own nationals; having our fate discussed by angry Albanians who surrounded us after one of their friends had been killed by the Italian troops; standing all night with no food or drink in a huddle by the sea; eventually being evacuated in a second attempt by the Italian Navy at 4.30 in the morning; enduring ten hours in the bowels of a battleship; suffering from dehydration (Heather collapsed and was carried off to the sickbay); being flown by a special BA flight to Heathrow where we were met by two anxious daughters (one heavily pregnant with our first grandchild); facing the blaze of floodlights and a barrage of microphones from the world media; being asked about our feelings, while all the time weeping for Albania. All this left us in a whirl of surrealism.

Then reality suddenly hit us.

What were we doing here in England's green and pleasant land? We were supposed to have stayed back there in Albania. We suddenly realised that we had not prayed when the orders came through to us telling us that we had to leave, as we had done earlier. We had not asked our church family what *they* felt the Lord wanted us to do. Like Peter we had reacted rather than responded to the situation.

Certainly, in all the clamour and chaos that had turned into confusion, and with our knee-jerk response, we felt that we had run away and forsaken our brothers and sisters.

It wasn't so much strike the shepherd and the sheep will scatter, but strike the sheep and the shepherds will flee. We'd done a disciple and run away. We'd proved to be a Peter – failing to keep our word under pressure. I now knew just how Peter felt. Weak when it comes to the crunch. And afterwards when it had all happened how he felt such a failure. I felt the same. And I also wept.

People under pressure, like us and Peter, get confused and need a safety net. Our emotions cry out for one.

Chapter 4

Needing a Net – Because of Him

But that's not the whole story. That's just one side. Yes, we need a net because of us, because of the unreliability of our own hearts and the uncertainties of our own emotions. But we also need a net (and I say this carefully) because we can't be too sure of Jesus. He was, and is, so unpredictable.

There are two kinds of unpredictability. First there is the sort of unpredictability that comes from *unreliability*. Unreliability is when you are never sure what someone is going to do because generally they aren't sure either. What they do or say one minute can change like the wind the next.

In one of my churches I had a young man who drove round town with a hand-made sign stuck in the back window of his car that said, 'The driver of this car may disappear at any moment at the sound of a trumpet.' That sign said more about his character than his theology of the second coming. At any moment he would just disappear, despite any promises he might have made to be somewhere or to do something. If the whim (or he called it 'leading') took him he wouldn't think of phoning to cancel his arrangements, he simply didn't turn up.

Unfortunately he was just like that. When I saw this sign appear in his car I asked, showing my exasperation with him and so maybe a little unkindly, 'Has anyone got a trumpet that I could blow?' I was fed up with his unreliability.

The unpredictability of Jesus wasn't like that. His was the unpredictability of otherness. He thought as God thinks – well he ought to, he was God. So what he did was *unexpected* rather than unreliable – just like God does the unexpected. Isaiah said something about this along the lines that God doesn't think or act like us, his thoughts and ways are light years away from ours. That was certainly true throughout the life of Jesus.

The contrast between human and divine planning was seen right at the start of his life here on earth. For example we read about 'wise men' choosing the humanly obvious path. A new king, to say nothing of a divine king, should be found in a palace in the capital. So off they trotted to talk to Herod the king of the region. But where does Jesus turn up? In a village. And when there was no room at the pub (Joseph's preferred choice) he is born in a animal shed. God spent his first night on earth in a food trough! On top of this we discover that these 'wise men' weren't God's first choice to see Jesus. He let a motley bunch of shepherds get there first after heaven broke through the stratosphere in excitement at Jesus' safe arrival.

What an odd and brief trailer for the Greatest Epic Ever Seen!

After a few songs and a personal announcement to this rag-tag bunch looking after their sheep on a hillside near Bethlehem and their on-the-spot decision to check the news out; after the star that few people noticed; after the arrival in a southern farming village of those celebrities who had come from the East; after the Spirit of God ing to a couple of nonagenarians in the Temple ...... the Deliverer's arrival; after a hasty journey to Egypt to escape the wrath of Herod, and a visit to the Temple at twelve, there was silence for thirty years.

No angelic advertisement campaign at the annual Passover saying 'He's coming. Who's coming? Watch this space.' All God had in mind was a hippy-type preacher down by a riverside who, a year or so before Jesus began his public ministry, started saying, 'Get your lives sorted out. Get ready for God's promised one.' What was the heavenly PR team up to (or *not* up to as the case may be!)? Preparations for Jesus and publicity for the occasion when he was to step onto the world stage were rather different from how our modern advertising agencies and image consultants would have handled them.

And when at the age of thirty he did eventually 'go public', Jesus himself was so unpredictable. At the start of his public life who did the King of the Universe choose as his close friends? Who did he choose to help him in his divine mission? Who did he choose to give the responsibility of carrying on his work when he was to return to heaven?Later when Jesus had gone back to heaven some three years after he began his ministry, the dons of the University of Jerusalem summed up Jesus' chief spokesmen as 'thick, uneducated northern fishermen'.

One of those who was destined to belong to the close circle of twelve followers of Jesus (and in fact later on was one of the seven who returned to Galilee with Peter), when he first heard about Jesus some three years earlier, initially reacted with similar scornful words of dismissal. He also held the common view that other people had about their northern region. 'Does anything good come out of Nazareth?' Nathaniel exploded.

Some weeks later after Nathaniel's outburst Jesus, out of the thousands who were interested in following him, chose twelve of the most unusual and incompatible people to be his closest companions.

Jesus always did the unexpected and unpredictable.

Who in their right mind would choose a friend of the High Priest's sacred family and an 'unacceptably unclean' tax collector; an intellectual and a couple of short-planked fishermen from up north; someone suffering from an inflated ego and another so shy that he wouldn't say 'boo to a goose'; an underground guerilla type and a collaborator with the occupying powers. These were the original Dirty Dozen!

And alongside this inner circle, who were the others that Jesus attracted and accepted? They were the rejects of society. Not the 'nice' people. No wonder the crowds came so readily and happily to Jesus. It was because he touched the untouchables (lepers and the like), ate with the unacceptables (fifth-columnist types called tax collectors), and welcomed the unrespectable (prostitutes and sinners). As far as society was concerned, most of Jesus' followers were the dregs, and failures of one kind or another. The best and most pure person in the world mixed with those who seemed to be the worst and most unpromising, and all he did was grin with delight when the 'establishment' called him 'The Failures' Friend'.

Jesus was so unpredictable.

Many times people, even his close friends, just stood back with open mouths saying 'Who on earth is this man?'

As I thought about this unpredictable Jesus I tried to put myself in the position of the disciples. I tried to think how they must have felt about Jesus, especially in those last days that preceded this lakeside encounter. Life for them was turning into an unpredictable whirlwind of events that seemed to get more and more out of control the closer they got to the vortex of the storm that centred on a hillside called 'Skull Mount' outside Jerusalem.

Earlier they'd got the green light from Jesus. Yes, he was the promised liberator. He was the king waiting in the wings, but he didn't make a very impressive entrance when he arrived at the capital on a donkey – a bit embarrassing that, something like the President of the United States of America arriving at Buckingham Palace in a Mini! Later he made a bit more of an impression when he went into the Temple courtyard and knocked over the money-changers' tables and caused some sheep and cattle to stampede. But, the next day, when people tried to crown him he blew it by disappearing behind some pillars in the colonnade of the Temple. What a missed opportunity!

Then, in the religious fervour of Passover night when feelings were running high for a new deliverer, at the time when Jerusalem was buzzing with expectation, instead of declaring himself he decides to go off and have a quiet meal with the twelve.

During the celebration meal with the twelve he makes it abundantly clear that they had a traitor in the camp and that he *knew* who it was, but he did nothing about it.

Then in the middle of the night he pops out secretly to a quiet hillside garden with his closest companions to have a prayer meeting! And to crown it all when the prayer time was interrupted, without any fuss he allows Judas (who turned out to be the traitor he'd spoken about) to reveal his identity to the soldiers with a kiss!

Things seemed for a moment or two to go 'his' way when the soldiers asked him who he was. When Jesus said that he was Almighty God they collapsed back on top of one another like some divine wind had hit them

and knocked them off their feet. It seemed as though
there was going to be a showdown at last when at that
point of divine intervention Peter produced a hidden
sword and took a swing at the nearest shadowy figure.
But then Jesus simply let the soldiers take him. At the
first sign of blood Jesus put a stop to the all too brief bit
of resistance put up by Peter by ticking him off, and to
add insult to injury he *healed* the only enemy casualty!
Finally, to cap it all, he said to his friends, 'If I wanted I
could call up ten thousand angels.' Then why in
heaven's name didn't he?

How confusing that someone who could heal incurables; with a word get rid of evil powers; stop a storm in
full flight; and even bring back to life people who were
dead (not just a matter of minutes but days later); *why*
then, in heaven's name, didn't he use all this power
when it was really needed?

Why, when the soldiers for a joke made a crown from
a thorny bramble and forced it on his head, *why* did he
take it? *Why*, when the crowd shouted out for his death
in the Roman Governor's courtyard and saw him bleed-
ing from his beating and that crown, *why* did he just
stand there? *Why*, when he was paraded before them
caricatured as some sort of a king with a cloak of royal
purple round his shoulders and a bulrush stuffed
between his tied hands like some sceptre of power, *why*
didn't he stun the crowd with his majesty like he had
surprised Peter, James and John up a mountain once?
Why didn't he let his face start to shine like the blazing
sun, and his blood-stained clothes glow as bright as
lightning? *Why* in fact didn't he simply walk across the
sea of people like he had a number of times walked
across the waves on the sea of Galilee? That would have
stopped them!

So unpredictable, this Jesus.

Why did he later pray for forgiveness for the soldiers
as they cruelly rammed those large iron nails through
his hands and feet? *Why* didn't he show the religious
leaders when they taunted him for being a rejected Son
of God, *why* when they made fun of him for saving
others but being impotent to set himself free, *why* didn't
he show them who he was and what he could do? *Why*
didn't he come down form the cross and let the world
see he really was the Promised One?

How was it possible for evil to get the better of good?

Can mere human beings stop God from being God?
Can they really kill off God?

Could the mocking demons, joining in with the jeer-
ing crowds, really get the better of God's Son?

Maybe he would surprise them at the end. Maybe
he'd show them who he was and what he could do with
a last-minute miracle. Everyone seemed to be holding
their breath for something like that – even the elements
seemed to pause in silence.

And then something did happen.

With a final gasp from his parched and dry throat he
croaked out with his last ounce of strength, 'It's done.
It's over.' And then his head dropped onto his chest and
he died.

Why? Why? Why? Why . . . ?

In some ways not only had *they* failed him but *he* had
failed them.

Sometimes, if we are absolutely honest with ourselves,
secretly deep down inside us we feel the same, though we
are scared to admit it in case God blows us to kingdom
come for doubting him. At times it's hard to hang on to
parts of the Bible that say things like David wrote in one
of his songs, 'Not one of your promises have failed.' If I'm
really truthful I have to admit that there have been a number of occasions when I have dared to say to God, 'That's

not true. Those promises haven't worked out. When I, or someone else in difficulties has really needed you God, it seems to me that you weren't there, despite saying that you'd be with us when we're up to our necks in deep water. When you promised that you'd act for the honour of your name, and you didn't, God, it's hard then to say that not one of your promises have failed!'

I recall that there was a time when, having tried to the best of my ability to honestly and faithfully teach God's word and tell what the Lord was doing in my own life, many of the influential members in one of my churches boycotted the services and withheld their offerings so as to make the finances of the church difficult. Despite praying so desperately for God to sort out that situation, instead of things getting better they got worse. A number in the choir refused to sing any new worship songs. Some stubbornly stayed seated while the congregation stood to sing, or they stomped out of the choir stalls. Finally, some of the trustees got together in an effort to get me removed from the church, almost causing my wife to have a nervous breakdown – she certainly had to have plenty of visits to the psychiatrist as a result.

Then later in Albania, where was the one who said, 'Those who honour me I will honour' when, despite the constant objections of one of our most faithful church members to her parents when they wanted to engage her to a man fifteen years her senior who wasn't a Christian, and contrary to her, and our, constant prayers, they still went ahead and did it. Everything that she felt God had been leading her into for her future just went up in smoke at that point.

Where was the Lord when a number of new young Albanian Christians read the promise, 'Seek and you will find, ask and it will be given to you, knock and the door will be opened up to you' as they, full of simple faith, prayed for spoilt relationships among the emerging leadership of our church to be healed, and they weren't healed and even got worse?

Where was the Lord 'who heals all your diseases' and says 'I am the one who heals you' when our sending church in the UK prayed for a young Dad in his thirties who was dying from a cancerous tumour of the brain (especially after God had healed another member a year or so earlier)? People had received lots of promises about him that just simply didn't happen.

Then what about us personally, when out of the blue our healthy and sporty twenty-eight-year-old daughter was diagnosed with an unusual and virulent form of cancer that raged from her stomach, to her bones, to her lymph glands and finally into her bone marrow in just eight weeks from the first sign of anything being wrong? Just four weeks after the final diagnosis of where the cancer was in her body, she died.

Where was God when thousands of people prayed for her, and churches gave us prophecies that God would do a last-minute miracle, and yet she relentlessly slid down the steep incline into death so quickly?

Where did God go to when she died and everything inside me died with her? Within a few months, I had sunk into a reactive depression and God seemed nowhere to be found.

There have been many occasions when I've had my doubts, but none like that last black hole. I now sympathised, and even joined in, with those who've said from the depth of their being, 'God has failed us.'

Of course, as a long-serving church leader and now fully fledged missionary, I knew in my head the *right* answers to give: 'Part of following Jesus is suffering for him.' 'We must differentiate between the presence of the Lord and a sense of the presence of the Lord.' 'God's prayer traffic lights have a positive green, an amber wait and a red no.' 'God doesn't heal all suffering here.' 'Healing is ultimately found in Heaven.' 'We can ask for anything – as long as it is the will of God', etc., etc., etc. . . . !' But knowing all the textbook answers didn't make things any easier; on the contrary, it only made things harder.

When the rubber hits the road sometimes it's hard to have faith.

Does that sound a bit like bad mouthing God?

Well, if it does, then all I can say is that David felt exactly like that and said so, as did lots of other people in the Bible. The one who wrote, 'None of your promises have failed me' also wrote, 'My God, why have you abandoned me?' In fact it seems as though, amazingly, even Jesus experienced the same sort of feelings as me. The Jesus who confidently said, after forewarning the disciples that they would all run away and leave him at crisis time, that despite everything his Father would always be with him, also felt abandoned by his heavenly Father.

I am glad that he understands how it is and how I feel because he had the same sort of experience as me. In desperation he cried out on his cross with the same words as David as he said, 'Father, oh my Father, where are you? Why have you left me alone?'

And that's just how these disciples felt in their time of confusion. Deserted. Let down. Totally confused.

Jesus, at times, just doesn't make sense.

How could the one who called a dead corpse out from a burial cave and into life less than five miles away and no more than a fortnight before, how could he who said at that time, 'I am the resurrection, I am that life', how could he now be dead, buried, and sealed away with official Roman seals inside his own burial cave?

The bottom of their world had fallen out, just like in those nightmares where you try to jump from one piece of cracking earth to another only to find it has moved or disappeared and you are falling, falling, falling down into nothingness and darkness. Would they wake up in a sweat like us before hitting the bottom – dead?

Their nightmare continued Friday night, all Saturday and into Sunday. A lifetime in a matter of hours.

And then. . .

Some over-emotional, over-imaginative women almost broke the door down on Passover Sunday morning, after an early morning visit to Jesus' grave, to say that they had found the stone moved from the entrance to the grave, the cave empty, and had seen an angel.

It needed some sensible men to prove them wrong!

Yet the stone *was* moved, the cave *was* empty, and this time not one or two, but a couple inside and a couple outside who stood guard there were – *angels!*

Later that day, the unpredictable Jesus did it again. Not only did he fold up his burial clothes and leave the place all tidy after being killed on the cross, but (something no one really expected or understood) he actually turned up in the garden of Joseph, the rich merchant from Aramathea, who had given up his unused family vault for Jesus' body. And there by the open grave he, Jesus himself, alive and well had talked face to face with a woman first. And not someone like his gracious and saintly mother, but an ex-prostitute, ex-demon-possessed woman called Mary from the red-light district of Magdala.

That certainly put the cat among the pigeons.

Maybe he had got the wrong Mary. No, but seriously, why her of all people?

Then, Jesus was everywhere. . .

. . .with a young married couple walking back home for an evening meal in their home in the village of Emmaus as they were heatedly taking sides about what had really happened that morning and who was right – the rational men or the emotional women.

. . .with ten of his close friends – suddenly appearing like the captain of the star ship *Enterprise* in the middle of a locked and bolted upstairs flat.

. . .also fitting in a private appearance to Peter somewhere.

Not only was he unpredictable about his appearances, but at times unrecognisable in his appearance. The couple on the road didn't realise that their fellow traveller was Jesus until a number of hours later – despite inviting him as a guest for the night into their home. It wasn't until he picked up a loaf of bread that was on the dinner table and lifted it up to thank God with the familiar Jewish blessing, 'Blessed are you, O Lord our God, King of the Universe, who brings forth bread from the earth. . .' Suddenly they recognised him, maybe they saw some nail marks in his hands, and then he was gone.

Mary, when she saw him, thought he was the gardener. But probably wet eyes didn't help her!

The ten thought he was a ghost suddenly materialising, and were terrified out of their tiny minds. They weren't too convinced either when he asked for some food and ate the only two things available – fish and honey. Who, after all, in their right minds would eat those two things together! But at least it proved he was real. Then just as they were getting used to this unexpected phenomenon, wooosh, faster than Paul Daniels, he was gone again.

Appearance on appearance, sometimes recognised and sometimes unrecognised.

Then nothing for a whole week!

Seven long days; 168 hours; 100,180 long minutes.

Once again they were beginning to think nothing was real (some things can be too good to be true) as each long minute ticked a slow march through that eternally long week, trampling all reality into the dust of doubt. Gradually fear and panic began to flood back in. Then just as though nothing had changed, out the blue Jesus appeared at their Sunday gathering which, as the previous week, was held in the familiar locked and bolted 'Top Room' of John Mark's Mum's house.

Now, what would you say is the best thing to do with frightened and confused people? Isn't it to tell them, 'Never mind', 'It's all right', 'Don't be frightened', etc.?

I remember one Christmas, as a small child, creeping downstairs to get an early and crafty peek at the presents round our small Christmas tree. As I opened the door something black with eyes of fire stirred in the dark room. In panic I fled up the stairs, but the ghostly shadow followed hard on my heels. With a shriek I dived into bed and trembled under the sheets as 'it' landed on me.

My parents rushed into the room at my howl of fear, and then laughed.

'It's okay,' they reassured me as the weight was lifted off the bed, 'Don't be frightened. Look.'

As I slowly emerged from the safety of my bed covers I saw the black 'something' in their arms. 'He's your Christmas present,' they explained, and offered the black phantom to me to hold. 'Don't be scared,' they told me, as a wet puppy tongue stretched out and licked me all over my face.

That's how fear should be dealt with, right?

But, what did the unpredictable Jesus do? Oh yes, he constantly repeated his, 'Shalom – Peace, to you' – but then every Jew said that as a normal everyday greeting!

Basically, he told them off for their lack of faith, lack of understanding and lack of spirituality. Then he gave them a thumping big Bible study starting at Genesis and ending at Malachi (thirty-nine books all told!) on the doctrines of Messianic Kingship and the resurrection! Well, that's what Dr Luke the psychologist says he did.

Quickly following on from this berating came his blessing. But once again he did something unpredictable. He went over to each one of them, blew into their faces, and said, 'Now breathe into your lives my spirit, my representative, the other me, the Holy Spirit.'

Then as soon as he did that, just as they were beginning to relax and feel strength flowing back into them, once again he was off.

All that appearing and disappearing was not only unsettling, it was unbearable. Their emotions swung from fear to faith, from despair to joy, from tears of sadness and frustration to tears of joy and all the way back again, and again, and again.

It was swings and roundabouts all at the same time.

It was like having a hot and cold shower in a sauna – supposed to tone you up but leaving you invigoratingly exhausted.

That's the unpredictable Jesus. You are never quite sure what he is going to do, what he is going to say, where he is going to turn up, even what he will look like.

But more of that later on.

So often Jesus did unexpected things in unexpected ways in unexpected places at unexpected times. And he still does.

There have been times when I have least expected to meet Jesus and he has caught me out and surprised me, sometimes frightening me like the disciples. I mentioned earlier when we were on holiday near York. One day, when planning to take the children out for a trip, we saw under the flap of our AA Road Map the brief description of a place that looked interesting, called Fountains Abbey. So off we went in the car, parked nearby and walked across the fields to see this historic monument – taking the usual tourist pictures on the way. As we entered the ruins of the Abbey and looked at the men repairing and making safe the walls, I walked up a slope to what would have been the elevated floor of the high altar. At that point, for safety reasons, the workmen had placed a length of scaffolding horizontally across the Abbey. I thought as I walked across to it that it looked a bit like a communion rail.

Suddenly – the Lord was there . . . but I don't know what the workmen must have thought.

Suddenly I was stopped in my tracks. The Lord was there. His presence was so powerful that I, as a very non-conformist non-conformist, felt I had to kneel on the grass in worship because the King of all the universe was there in a special way.

I don't know what the workmen thought. Maybe they thought that they had dropped a hammer or that something else had fallen down on my head and hit me – which in a way it had. There on the grass I wasn't aware of anything or anyone else, just the Lord of Glory meeting me in the ruins of an old abbey.

Is that unpredictable or what?!

Well, I suppose we were at a 'holy' site. But what about the time when I was simply walking down the road of a most respectable and upper-class village, returning to the house where I was staying while on a three-month sabbatical? Suddenly I found myself standing under a beautiful almond tree in full blossom, with tears in my eyes saying, 'Jesus I love you, I love you, I love you.' Not the most usual thing that one sees these days!

Jesus meeting you personally and powerfully as you are minding your own business and quietly walking along an ordinary road . . . now *that's* not safe!

Neither was the time when a middle-aged atheist I knew was cycling home from work. Furiously peddling away he was arguing within himself about the way that Jesus, through the constant witness to their faith of some of his workmates, was challenging him to acknowledge the reality of Jesus and trust him. As he cycled along the road he was literally thrown – no, not *blown* as there was no wind that day – into a ditch where he found himself sobbing about the wrongs he had done and asking Jesus to come into his life to forgive and change him. A modern 'Saul on the road to Damascus' experience.

People ask: does God really do such unexpected things that might embarrass us?

In one word: Yes!

So the problem is, not only that we need a safety net because of ourselves and our own emotional state, but we also need a safety net because of what Jesus is like, and what he does. The 'Following Jesus' package that preachers at times glibly give away Sunday by Sunday in their sermons ought to include a clear warning – like the warning on those cigarette packets in the UK, which is cynically missing from the cigarettes people are encouraged to buy here in Albania for less than 25p a packet. Following Jesus is *not* safe, enquirers should be told.

In fact with Jesus nothing, and no one, is safe because in the comfortable sense of the word, he isn't. The famous and well-worn phrase on the lips of all Narnia fans is, 'Aslan is not a tame lion.' It's all very well to say, like David in one of his songs, 'The Lord is my refuge and strength', but at times we need a safety net to secure us when the Lord calls us, like Peter, to walk on the water. Many times Jesus isn't safe to follow or be with.

David in another song may well have written, 'I may fall but the Lord holds on to me.' But there are those occasions when even though the Lord has assured us that he has got a firm hold of us, his arms seem to be so very elastic that we appear to keep on plunging downwards like someone on a bungee rope.

That's why, after all the crisis and crash of faith at the cross, the confusion, unreality, and unpredictability of everything after Easter Sunday, Peter said words to the effect that, 'Enough is enough. I can't stand all this coming and going. I'm going back to the security and predictability of fishing.'

Chapter 5

Three Men in a Boat or Personalities in Need of a Safety Net

The man who initiated the fishing expedition in the *Jesus Story Book* that John wrote was Peter.

But who was this Peter? What sort of character was he?

Peter was a born leader. I guess from earliest childhood days he was the sort who said, 'Let's play football!' and everyone straight away said, 'Peter, Peter. I want to be on your side, Peter, choose me!' If he said, 'Today, we are going to be fishermen, like Jimmy and John's dad', then immediately Andrew, Peter's kid brother, would trot off to return post haste with string, bent pins, and a bucket held tight to his chest. Why the bucket? Well, if Peter said that they were going to be fishermen, then they would certainly need a bucket for all the fish they would be bound to catch. They would end up with *loads* of fish. Peter knew a thing or two when it came to fishing!

Because others looked up to Peter, he became a very confident, self-assured sort of person. In fact at times he became a bit too cock-sure and could be a bit bossy – in the nicest sense of the word of course.

People who are sure of themselves generally make a success of most things, and because of that, they aren't afraid to make a fool of themselves either. They usually can carry it off whatever happens.

Peter was basically what we would call an *extrovert*. Extroverts make great pioneers, great adventurers, great risk-takers, and are great at sharing their faith. They are natural evangelists. They are up-front people.

And they are enthusiasts. Either they are enthusiastically *in* or they are totally *out*. With them it is one thing or the other. Extroverts aren't the sort of people who are embarrassed to let others know which side they are on.

And yet below the surface of Peter's extrovertness he was a very private person - though to look at him you wouldn't have thought so. But then bright lights always do create dark shadows. Despite appearing to be unaffected by peoples' criticisms, Peter secretly felt a lot and could actually be deeply hurt.

Nevertheless, Peter always gives off an air of bluff confidence whenever you meet him in the Bible. He was always first in the queue of volunteers. When Jesus needed a boat for a trip or a pulpit, it was certain to be Peter's. When Jesus wanted a volunteer Peter was always first to offer his services. When Jesus asked a question, Peter was always the one to pop up with an answer, even if it was the wrong one.

Peter was ready to spend time in prayer with Jesus even if it might mean climbing up to the top of a mountain while the others (apart from James and John) preferred to relax down at the bottom in the shade. Because of his readiness on that occasion to accompany Jesus, Peter was rewarded with a foretaste of Jesus' eternal glory. The longer Jesus prayed, the more the whole of his personality seemed to become more alive until it looked as though he started to shine. It was as if his divinity couldn't keep hidden as he prayed. The face of Jesus ended up shining like the sun. Even his clothes became whiter than any modern washing powder could produce or boast. That's just how Peter described it to young John Mark when he was collecting stories for his *Jesus Biography*.

In the emotion of the moment the 'self-assured' Peter later explained to Mark how he foolishly started to make plans for Jesus and began to tell everyone what to do.

'Let's make this a holy place,' he had blurted out. 'We can make three shrines. One for Moses and one for Elijah' (two historical figures who both literally turned up 'out of the blue' to have a chat with Jesus about *his* future plans for saving the world – something that would be a bit like another 'exodus' Moses said). 'The biggest and best shrine will be for you, Jesus,' Peter proudly announced.

The ideas were tumbling out. He was on a roller now.

'And let's all be like hermits,' he probably added. 'Let's all live here on this mountain where we can enjoy a bit of heaven on earth.'

Of course he was just letting his mouth off because he couldn't cope with such a mind-blowing experience, but being the extrovert that he was he had to say something.

It was the same when he got a ten out of ten from Jesus for getting the right answer about who Jesus really is. But then rather than being content with getting that first bit right he blew the whole thing by starting to reorganise Jesus' plans. As soon as Jesus agreed with Peter that he was the Son of God and the promised deliverer he spoilt it for Peter by adding that as such he would be betrayed, arrested and killed off. Peter immediately jumped in without thinking and said, 'Never.' At which point Jesus firmly told him that having tuned in onto God's wavelength earlier, now he was on the Devil's frequency.

Then, as the extrovert that he was, there was Peter's classic leap of faith that got him into deep water (literally). It happened one stormy night, just before dawn, when Jesus met the lonely frightened disciples 'mid ocean' on the sea of Galilee. They all thought that what they saw emerging through the lightning-illuminated sky was a ghost. After all it's not normal to see someone walking on water in the middle of a huge lake!

Jesus, to cheer them up, said, 'Don't be scared, it's me.' To which Peter, once again without thinking, said, 'Okay Jesus, if it is you, give me half a chance and I'll come and join you on the water.' That was bad enough, but to make matters worse Jesus took him up on his offer and gave him an invitation to put his feet where his mouth was and come and join him.

Well, Peter had to maintain his credibility and pride (after all if everything else failed at least he was a strong swimmer) so he cautiously eased himself over the side of the boat. When he got out he found that the water was sort of soggy and that it was no worse than walking on soft mud. In the flush of excitement and success, and maybe thinking how 'water-walking' would look good on his CV (might even one day make him into Saint Peter), he got a bit over-confident and started to swagger over to Jesus.

It wasn't too long before reality sank in and he suddenly realised what he was thoughtlessly doing. And at that point he slowly started to sink.

Up to his neck in deep water, with his heavily sodden night fishing clothes pulling him yet further down, he eventually had to forget his pride and call out for Jesus to rescue him.

Once Jesus had grabbed him and brought him back in the boat, I guess it didn't take too many minutes before his extrovert personality bounced back. Probably he thought to himself, 'Well, at least I did it for a while, I walked a bit on water. Not bad for a start.'

What with 'water walking', healing a few sick people (after Jesus had given them all the power to do this), and delivering a few more people from the power of evil spirits (all these things proudly displayed on his brain like medals on a war-veteran's chest), later, when Jesus was on the road up to Jerusalem and again started to talk about his imminent suffering and death, once more the buoyantly confident, self-assured nature of Peter bobbed up. This time he didn't say, 'Never, not you', but, 'Okay, but I'll stand by you.' And he really meant it.

A day or so later Peter repeated his intention. At their last meal together Jesus warned his disciples that as soon as he, their leader, was arrested they would all run away to fend for themselves and leave him on his own. Peter confidently bragged, 'The others might . . . but not me. You can count on me, Jesus. I'll die for you.' Even when Jesus warned him bluntly that a time of supernatural battle was coming when he would say that he had nothing to do with Jesus, and that Peter would even go so far as to say that he didn't know who Jesus was, Peter indignantly protested with a resounding 'Poo!'

Despite his initial objections Peter probably did, on reflection, take some of Jesus' warning to heart (he'd show Jesus that he was no coward). We find out that it was Peter who had secreted a short-bladed sword under his coat before they went across town to the garden where Jesus frequently prayed. It was Peter who, like some bodyguard, stayed close to Jesus later that night as he prayed alone under the olive trees. It was Peter who lashed out, one against a squadron of soldiers who came to arrest Jesus, and drew the only blood that night. Pity it was only the High Priest's servant, and only an ear! But Peter was 'the defender of the faith'. Or did he just panic?

Yet not long after, in contrast to this brief show of bravery (or maybe because of it), only a matter of hours later, he was using his old fisherman's language to enforce the fact to some soldiers that he was no follower of this gentle Galilean. It was there, in the High Priest's courtyard, in the eerie flickering light thrown out by the open fire that a young girl caught him on the hop with a simple statement: 'You're from up north, like him in there, aren't you? You're not with *him*, are you?'

Peter could fight a soldier but couldn't answer a girl. 'No way. I don't know the man,' he replied, denied and (after three times) went out and just as violently cried. His self-assurance was suddenly shattered by a cockerel's third attempt to tell the world that morning was coming. All at once Peter remembered that this was the sign Jesus had given to him in the upstairs room to warn him of the danger he was going to be in. The glance of Jesus from the porch at the same moment as the cock crowed went like a sword into Peter's very guts and disembowelled all his self-confidence.

Yes, Peter the extrovert could hurt and be hurt.

In fact when he so badly let Jesus down and Jesus from the verandah of the High Priest's home turned towards him, and caught his eye as if to say, 'Yes, I heard all that', at that raw moment of denial Peter could do nothing but shoot out into the secrecy of the night and sob his heart out.

Who would have thought it! The tough fisherman of Capernaum, the Rambo of Galilee, crying.

But, I can understand Peter's reaction. I spent days crying over Albania and the fact that we had left our friends to face suffering alone. However, more than that I cried at the thought of letting Jesus down. Tears welled up from a mixture of pain for others, shock at what had happened, guilt for disobedience, and a deep sense of failure – despite one or two of the people in our village saying we should not stay in our home in Albania.

The picture of neighbours and church members in tears, some of whom had risked danger to come and see us off, will always be burned into my mind, just like the eyes of Jesus turning on Peter.

Thankfully our situation wasn't as devastating as some other missionaries who were forcefully told, 'If you leave us now, don't bother to come back'; 'Why do you come to help us when life is easy, but when it gets tough and we really need you, you forsake us?'; 'If that is what your gospel is about, then we don't want it.' At least a couple of our members had come to us the night before we left and said that we should go, and whatever we eventually did the majority of our church not only knew about but understood the orders we had been given.

Our problem arose first from the agony of seeing the country we loved fall apart into anarchy and bloodshed, but then also (and more importantly) our sadness stemmed mainly from the fact that we felt that we shouldn't have left. It wasn't a matter of self-confidence breaking down but the feeling that we had gone against a clear sense (which had increased in us more and more like the gunfire that multiplied around us in the days preceding our evacuation) that God wanted us to stay. Sadly, our resolve had broken down.

What gave way for Peter was everything that he had confidently built on and around a fatal 'fault line', just like Californians in San Francisco and Los Angeles have done on the San Andreas Fault. Only, Peter's 'fault line' was something internal that he had in his character. It was called 'self-confidence'.

Self-confidence is good up to a point as long as we remember that 'self' is flawed and certain to crack at some time. But the higher self-confidence rises, or the more we build on it, the harder the fall of 'failure' becomes.

And now down by the beach Jesus opened up that recent and still raw wound. Once again Peter experienced a stab of pain when Jesus asked him about the depth and reality of his commitment and care.

Yes, extroverts do feel things despite their tendency to appear insensitive to others. They feel things deeply, but they have to put on a brave face for the sake of appearances. They can't let the side down.

*   *   *

Next on the list of returnees for this Lake District fishing trip was Thomas – an odd second in command.

Tom was a twin. We don't know anything about his other half, whether he had a brother or sister. We don't know whether his twin was interested in Jesus or not. We know absolutely nothing – which is strange because twins generally do things together.

In the church I went to as a young teenager we had two sisters who were twins – identical twins. How they led everyone a merry dance. They looked alike, dressed alike, had interests alike, and went to the local grammar school together. They both wanted to teach. They even managed to get into the same teacher training college. And to crown it all, they both had a similar sense of mischief.

As students at school they enjoyed doing crazy things like swapping lessons and homework. Then as they grew up they had fun swapping boyfriends (who got so confused). Later on, at teacher training college when given teaching placements, they even swapped their 'placement' schools for a couple of days without anyone knowing.

So, if twins do things together, where was Tom's twin?

*They looked alike, dressed alike, had interests alike . . . And
. . . they both had a similar sense of mischief*

We don't even know if his twin was alive or dead. Of
course with the risks to health in those days it was very
possible that his twin had died, and if so, as twins are so
close emotionally, that may have affected Tom's
personality.

In our village in Albania by the side of the road, on the
wall that surrounds the brick factory that gives our village one of its names ('NishTulla' – translated 'Brick
Factory'), there is a plaque with flower holders either
side full of plastic flowers set up in memory of a twelve-
year-old boy called Kastriot.

Kastriot was one of two twins who came to our
church services with other members of his family. His
death happened one day during the period when we
were evacuated to England. He was tragically killed by
a car crushing him against the wall of the brick factory
as he and his twin brother were cycling together, with
one of their friends, on the narrow road that goes
through our village to the local school.

Korab, the twin who was left, has been emotionally
scarred by his brother's death. He has dull eyes and cries

alone with the pain of losing his other half. He has
shrunk into a shell of insecurity, just like a snail disap-
pears when something has touched it. God only knows
how he will grow up, and what damage to his character
he will carry into the future. He is already creating a
safety net. The safety net of withdrawal.

If that was Thomas's experience (losing his twin, I
mean) it would go a long way in explaining some of his
personality traits.

Whether that was the cause or not we will never
know, but Thomas certainly comes across as a *pessimist*,
and at times even a fatalist. He had exactly the same
advantages of the other eleven. He heard the same
teaching, saw the same miracles, shared the same calling, experienced the same power of Jesus, and now felt
the same pain and confusion of all the others, yet he
reacted so differently.

Tom comes to our notice a number of times in the
Bible accounts of the life of Jesus.

We read about his call, along with all the other apostles,
after Jesus had spent a night of prayer sorting out
who, from the hundreds following him, were the right
ones to choose to be his close friends and later represen-
tatives when he left earth to return to heaven. The next
time we read about him he reacts very pessimistically
when Jesus explains that he wants to make a visit to a
bereaved family of friends who had asked for his help
and who lived near the capital city of Jerusalem. When
Thomas heard about this invitation, with a sinking heart
he felt it his duty to remind Jesus of the opposition that
they had experienced there last time and how the religious leaders had tried to kill Jesus by throwing stones at
him.

'Should we really be going back there, Jesus? Is it sensible? Is it safe?' he asked glumly.

Jesus cryptically replied that there were a few limited hours of daylight in which to work. In other words, there was a small window of opportunity open that would soon be closing, and to miss God's timing now would result in a greater misfortune.

Thomas, anyway, couldn't see anything else but disaster round the corner – despite Jesus talking about his power over death and the need for their faith to be expanded.

Fatalism rather than faith was his mind-set, and they are two very different things.

Every day we hear a Turkish word that's used a great deal in our village. It's used as a blanket cover for most things that happen in life. 'Kismet,' people say. If good happens – it's kismet. If bad happens – it's kismet. Everything happens depending on how the dice falls. It's fate, it's fortune, it's the will of Allah.

And that was Thomas's pessimistic point of view when Jesus told them that he would be going to his friend, Lazarus's, house.

'If he's got to go, he's got to go. He's walking into a death trap, but I suppose we have to go with him "into the valley of death . . ." and all that! After all everyone has to die sometime. So when he dies we'll just go along in a sort of suicide pact and die with him. It's probably all in the Plan. You can't alter that.'

That's not faith, that's fatalism.

It was that same sort of fatalistic negativism that Thomas showed when, after washing their feet, Jesus explained that he was going to leave them so as to get a place ready for all his followers, a place where they would live happily ever after.

'You know what I'm talking about,' said Jesus, after having explained for the 'nth' time about his death, resurrection and going up into heaven afterwards.

'No, we don't,' chipped in Thomas. 'We don't know where you are going, so we can't know about the way to get there. How can we? Once again I, and I think I speak for the majority, just don't understand what you're on about, Jesus.'

What an encouragement Thomas must have been to Jesus!

I know the same sort of sinking feeling that Jesus must have had. After having preached my heart out at some service or other, it's so sad to have someone shake my hand at the door of the church and to hear them say, 'Lovely service', showing that they really hadn't understood a word of the message that was about the need for radical change. Or, more depressingly someone might say 'I really don't know what you were on about today. It was as clear as mud.'

Maybe for Thomas the inevitability and pain of death hung like a spectre over him, and that was what darkened his mind.

Finally of course there is that classic line which ever since has dubbed him, and every other unconvinced sceptic, as a 'Doubting Thomas'. It was what Thomas said on one of those 'Here-he-is-Where's-he-gone?' occasions that gave him the nickname of 'The Doubter'.

Jesus had already met ten of the twelve by beaming into their padlocked 'upper room', greeted them as though nothing had happened, showed them his hands and side, ate some fish and honey, blew in their faces and mentioned something about the Holy Spirit, then abruptly said, 'See you', and suddenly vanished. Thomas turned up late, heard their garbled and excited account, and reproachfully shook his head in disbelief. But then I ask myself, would I have believed people who told me something like that, even if there were ten of them?

Thomas's reaction was typically pessimistic and blunt.

'Unless I can see him for myself with my own two eyes; unless I can feel him for myself and know it's him by putting this finger of mine right into the holes made in his hands by those thick Roman iron nails; unless I put my hand between his ribs where the spear went into his heart, I can't, and I won't, be convinced that dead people live! Jesus can't be alive.'

No wonder the following week he fell at Jesus' feet and gasped out those words, 'My Lord and my God.' He got more than he bargained for when Jesus called him over and repeated word for word what he demanded as a sign of the reality of Jesus' resurrection. In fact I wonder about that previous Sunday. Was Jesus still in the room staying there all the time while Thomas had his say? Maybe all that had happened was that he had become invisible to the naked eye. He hadn't really gone, he'd just disappeared!

How devastating all this was to Thomas and his pessimism.

Pessimists need a safety net – a big bit of reassurance.

My Dad, unlike his usually optimistic self, was strangely pessimistic about a rowing boat he had made for me when I was a child. On one of his 'days off' from work we had worked on it together, making something that looked more like a punt with two planks of wood (6ft long by 1ft deep) curved off at both ends and then undergirded with a sheet of 6x4 hardboard. Two seats were screwed inside and a plywood floor fixed into place, and finally on the outside the bottom was painted with bitumen and the sides given a coat of bright red gloss paint.

The next Saturday, when the boat and the oars were all finished and dry, we went down to the beach with it tied on to the car roof to try it out – only we did it at dusk, in the local paddling pool, so that no one could see if it sank.

It didn't. And despite people saying that by the laws of ship building it should last no more than six months, it was still going strong eight years later when we, with a touch of sadness, sold it as a tender for an eighteen foot motorised sailing boat that my Dad also owned.

Dad's pessimism proved false, but on that occasion he felt that he needed a huge 'safety margin' – just in case!

Dusk and a two-foot deep paddling pool was his safety net.

For some pessimists it's the 'Let's-try-it-but-not-let-anyone-else-see' precaution. For others it's the qualifying 'I-knew-it-couldn't-be-true, I-knew-it-wouldn't-happen' opt out clause. Or it's their fatalistic 'It-was-meant-to-be' or 'What-will-be-will-be' net.

Optimists and pessimists both have nets.

. . . to try it out – only at dusk, in the local paddling pool, so that no one could see if it sank.

* * *

Next in line, in this fugitives' group, there was Nathaniel.

There's not a lot you can say about Nathaniel as he only turns up two or three times in the Bible. The first time is in a brief account of when Jesus first crossed his path. Next he is simply named in Jesus' 'honours list' of special disciples, and finally we come across him here at the lakeside incident. But his main claim to fame comes in the short passage that describes how he first met Jesus. Though short those few lines say a lot about this man.

I call Nathaniel the *rationalist*. Nat was the thinker in the group, or that's how he appears to me when I read about him on the first occasion that he met Jesus. Sitting in the shade of a fig tree, he was thinking through the matter of hope, or lack of it, in their occupied, subjugated and oppressed nation. His conclusion was that their only hope would be found in the promised deliverer, the Messiah, the one sent by God.

In a similar way the Alliance of Albanian Evangelical Churches came to the same conclusion for the devastated nation of Albania. One year on after the 1997 national uprising which led to anarchy, left chaos, created more poverty and unemployment, destroyed infra-structures, and caused blood feuds and fear (at that time we were still regularly going to bed to a lullaby of dogs barking, cats howling and machine guns chattering), the Evangelical Churches agreed together to have as the theme for a live televised Easter United Celebration in the capital, 'Jesus, the only hope for Albania.'

That was the logical answer that Nathaniel came to for his own people, Israel, nearly two thousand years before. 'We need the hope-giver.'

As he was mulling this thought of 'hope' over in his mind, three of his mates came back to his village all excited and said, 'You know the one that Moses and all the prophets wrote about in the Bible, the one to come and free Israel? Well, we've found him. His name is

Jesus and he comes from the village opposite, from Nazareth.'

Thinking of the reputation of Nazareth, Nat did a quick mental calculation as he checked off all the promises about the Messiah and the many rebel upstarts who had come from that region. His logic led him to one conclusion. Dismissively he replied, 'Not Nazareth. No lasting leader of any real influence comes from there. Nazareth is not biblically or demographically an important, or good enough place.'

Nathaniel would have made either a strong fundamentalist in theology, or a good lecturer in sociology.

But in fact he was jumping to conclusions.

Philip, cut through his logic with the only effective argument for people with such a mind-set. 'Come and have a look,' he challenged him.

Although many rationalists and a number of scientists still criticise Christians for what they call an unsubstantiated 'leap in the dark', they in fact do the same. It's just that they don't jump as far. And when they do, they call their arguments 'logical steps' or 'extrapolations'.

When Jesus saw Nathaniel coming to meet him, without introducing himself, Jesus went to the root of the matter and straight into Nathaniel's heart with a pun. 'Here is one of Israel's seekers after truth. A man who won't make a decision, be deceived (literally 'be a Jacob') or be swayed one way or another without knowing all the facts.'

'How do you know what I'm like?' Nathaniel answered, suspiciously logical to the end. 'We haven't even met yet.'

Then Jesus said something weird.

'I was watching you, and I could see what you were thinking about, before Philip got round to asking you to come and meet me. You were sitting under a fig tree thinking about Jacob, the deceiver, becoming Israel and God's chosen prince. You were thinking about false and true hopes.'

In for a penny, in for a pound, Nathaniel rationally concluded. Somewhat overcome by the realisation that Jesus seemed to be able to read his secret thoughts, Nat launched into one of the first great statements of faith to be made about Jesus. 'You're a wise teacher, you must be the king Israel needs. You're the Son of God.'

'On such flimsy evidence?' Jesus benignly smiled. 'You say I'm all this because I told you about what was on your mind in your special 'thinking place'. You've not seen anything yet. You'll have your own 'Jacob's ladder' experience when you see heaven opened and the angels going up and down all around me.'

Nathaniel was now totally convinced.

Thinkers, once convinced, become one hundred percenters.

But then, on the other hand, thinkers can also be convinced a second time – in the opposite direction! Meg (not her real name) was one of my young people in the early days of my ministry in the UK. She had grown up in a Christian family, knew the Christian faith well, but more importantly she had her own personal experience of Jesus. She always wanted to know answers to her questions whether at school or in church. When she was convinced about something, she always followed through by arguing the case with others.

As a teenager all alone she sometimes spoke up for her faith at school. She also joined the 'door knockers' team in our church who did cold visits (yes, in winter they were – but not that sort of cold visit) to talk to people that we had never met before about the Lord Jesus. Eventually she went to Bible College where she ended up with an excellent honours degree (better than me with my BD failed!)

and eventually worked with a London church witnessing to Muslim women about the Christian faith.

Throughout the early days of her life she led many people to Jesus. But then she went to an Arab country to work in secular employment. Initially she saw this as an opportunity to tell people in a land closed to the Christian message about the Lord Jesus. But while she was there, for some reason, she started to have second thoughts about her faith. Now, this once happy liberated Christian is a sad, law-bound, veiled Muslim woman. How come? Why? I really don't know.

Maybe the problem is that thinkers like to neatly tie up all the loose ends – which is something that you can't do with God. The longer I've been a Christian the more I've come to reluctantly admit that there's a lot in this life, and the next, and a great deal about God that I don't understand. Maybe that was Nathaniel's problem after the resurrection of Jesus. He had too many things that he just couldn't get his head round.

So, the man who had left Galilee to follow Jesus, now, despite everything that he had heard, had seen, and everything that he had understood, was returning with the others up north, making his way back home, totally confused. Maybe he was disappointed because he hadn't yet seen the angels ascending and descending on Jesus!

Returning to his old predictable life was safer than the uncertainty of the new.

Rationalists can at times be conveniently irrational.

Chapter 6

Four More for the Boat

Whatever the scientific advances of the twentieth century, and people calling it the 'Technological Age', the end of the twentieth century and the beginning of the twenty-first might better be called the 'Age of Subjectivism and Feelings'.

Constantly people are being encouraged to take an in-depth look at their feelings. They are expected to hang them out for all (not just the psychiatrist/psychoanalyst) to see, just like we used to do with our washing every Monday before someone invented the tumble dryer. There it was, all the week's washing hung out on the line in the garden.

Interviewers on the TV or radio no longer say, 'What do you *think* about. . . ?' but 'What do you *feel*. . . ?'

We stumbled out of the VIP lounge at Heathrow Airport, physically tired and emotionally exhausted at the end of our traumatic evacuation. It had been over thirty-eight hours since leaving our village in Albania and landing in the UK – thirty-six of those without food and drink until British Airways gave us chicken and champagne on our homeward flight from Italy.

As we were confronted by the glare of the TV lights that blazed down on us outside the lounge door, the first question the press threw at us, with their thrusting microphones vying for pole position, was, 'What are your feelings about Albania and your experience there?'

'What I feel is what I am', would be an appropriate modern dictum.

I must have what I feel I need – I must have what I want. Feelings rule OK!

As I write, Selwyn Hughes comments on how society has changed to this position in his current booklet *Every Day with Jesus* on the Psalms. In the introduction he records how thirty-five years ago in a culture of rationalism and scientific knowledge he used to write a lot about the fact that we are *feeling* beings as well as *thinking* beings. 'Now our culture has done a 180 degree turn,' he says. 'In this postmodern age the emphasis is on subjective feelings – if it feels right, do it. Thinking has now given way to feeling.' To redress the balance he explains how these days he writes more about the fact that what we *think* affects the way we feel.

Look around. So many things today are judged exclusively by the 'Feel-good' Factor.

If Peter was the egoist (the self-confident extrovert), Thomas the pessimist, and Nathaniel the rationalist, then what can we say about the next in the list, John?

In the strictest sense of the word we could call John the *emotionalist* (that is: someone who is sensitive, temperamental, passionate). John was a man who throughout his life showed passion.

He *felt* anger towards those who rejected his Jesus. On one occasion he and his brother earned the name 'The Thunderers'. Jesus gave them that name because they demanded that he should allow them to call down fire from heaven like Moses and Elijah. 'Blast them to bits', was their passionate response. Of course it helped that the people who didn't want Jesus were Samaritans –

those foreign immigrants next door that no self-respecting Jew got on with!

He *felt* injured pride after he and his brother had surreptitiously sidled up to Jesus one day when the thirteen of them were out for a walk. He quietly asked Jesus for special privileges in the coming kingdom ('I'll be Prime Minister and James can be Chief Whip,' he suggested). When the rest found out about these two brothers' unprofessional conduct, it certainly caused a right old ding dong in the inner circle. John in turn got annoyed because he was found out and because he didn't get what he wanted – that special favour for a special friend! He *felt* offended.

He *felt* the sort of pride that pushes others around. 'Hey, Jesus. We saw this exorcist, and of all the cheek, he was getting rid of evil spirits in your name,' John informed Jesus one day. 'He's not one of us, so we told him to stop or we'd be after him for breach of copyright. We're the only ones in direct apostolic succession who can officially use your name, aren't we?'

He *felt* over-confident. When Jesus asked if John and his brother could drink the poisoned chalice of suffering, and go under the waves of death for him, John, without batting an eyelid, said 'Yes, of course we can.'

He *felt* he could cope with anything thrown at him.

But in reality he also *felt* overwhelmed by this Jesus. When as a 'thank-you' present for using his boat as a pulpit Jesus told Peter where to find a netful of fish and both the boats of Peter and John nearly sank with the catch, they all gawped at Jesus (John included) and in amazement they whispered to each other, 'Who on earth is this man we've got mixed up with?'

Above all he *felt* love. He loved Jesus.

Sadly in many parts of the world today the thought of that word 'love' creates many sorts of negative vibes that are to do with homosexuality. But, as I said earlier, in Albania we have come to understand things from a more biblical perspective, as the two cultures are in so many ways similar. Men, who are real men, aren't afraid of, ashamed about, or misunderstood for, showing proper affection to one another. It's the most natural thing to us now to see a car stop all the traffic around it at a road junction or non-functioning set of traffic lights, as the male driver leans out to kiss the policeman on point duty on both cheeks – four times!

I remember the first time one of the Albanian drivers from our mission centre placed his hand on my knee at a cross roads, gave it a squeeze and with genuine concern asked, 'Are you worried about anything?' In my best British way I had been sitting quietly in the vehicle letting him concentrate on his driving (you need 200 per cent attention on Albanian roads) while I was lost in my own thoughts. I almost panicked as his hand landed on me and felt like saying, 'Worried? Worried about anything? Yes I am. It's your hand on my knee.' But quickly I remembered that I was in a different culture and told myself how people do things differently here. Over the years I have come to learn that men here can quite happily express emotion without any hidden agenda.

Not only did John love Jesus but he was loved by Jesus. In fact he was nicknamed the 'disciple of love' probably because he used the word 'love' forty-seven times in his gospel, and thirty-seven times in his letters (I found that out on my computer). Sadly in these modern days we are controlled more and more by a Western mind-set in which the true idea of love has been devalued, corrupted and defiled. John White was right to entitle his book *Eros Defiled*.

For our twenty-fifth wedding anniversary (eight years ago now) someone sent us an article entitled 'We are the survivors' – a humorous comment for those whose marriages had kept going throughout, and in spite of, all the changes in society. And how society has changed! When we were on a visit to England a few years ago my wife tried to find a congratulations card for a Golden Wedding Anniversary – the true long distance runners – but she had some real difficulty. There were more cards in the shop that were commiserating with or congratulating people on their divorce than Golden Anniversary cards.

He placed his hand on my knee at a crossroads, gave it a squeeze and asked, 'Are you worried about anything?'

Love really isn't understood much today, and so doesn't last long. Perhaps it's considered to be just another part of the disposable society in which we live. Sadly the genuine thing is hard to find – it's an endangered species of flora – and when it is seen blossoming in its beautiful and fragile simplicity, people tend to trample on it by talking about it in terms of 'naivety'.

True love is great, but as such it does open you up to pain. Love, and you can be hurt – a lot. But that seems to be part of this package of tender emotions.

And there is nothing so painful as love lost.

One day sobs and sniffles reverberated around the bedroom of our youngest daughter. The boy she had been going out with for three years had decided to end his relationship with her for another girl. The most painful thing for our daughter was the fact that it was for a friend of hers. More than likely we can all sympathise. Who hasn't had a broken heart over lost love, or love slighted? Most of us have signed up for The Broken Hearts Club at one time or another. The lovely thing was her reaction. When the friend came to stay in the area our daughter loaned her one of her best dresses to go out in with her ex. But of more interest was the spiritual   lesson she learned. 'This must feel a bit like it was for Jesus. How much worse for him after all his love for us . . . and then not to be wanted,' was her conclusion.

After she had gone through a sort of pain barrier – the pain of letting him go – he eventually realised that the other girl wasn't the girl for him, returned, and eventually married our daughter. And now we have a lovely grandson. End of a bumpy but ultimately happy episode in their all too short marriage – as she was to die of cancer before their ninth wedding anniversary.

Bravely, in her last days in hospital she was heard to say to couples who were having relationship problems, with her usual mischievous and cheeky smile on her face, 'Hey, you two, you have to respect me 'cos I'm very, *very* sick. So, listen to me.' Then she would gently but firmly sock it to them with the punch line, 'Value one another, because you don't know how long you've got together.'

However, in the middle of that earlier experience when she thought that she had lost him, it was nothing but pain for her. And now for us who still love her, and have been separated from her, we are experiencing a similar yet different sort of pain. It is painful, this love thing.

So it was for John. The one he had come to understand, follow, admire, and care for, now was gone. He was killed in a most cruel and prolonged way – strung up on a cross to die, half suffocating and slowly dehydrating. Even in those last moments before he died on the cross Jesus saw John's capacity for love as he turned to his own mother, Mary, and John, who were both standing at the foot of his cross, and said, 'Mother, let John be a substitute son. John, look after Mary as though she were your own mother.'

Love, loved and loving, to the last.

And with that Jesus died and was buried.

'So what now?' John must have thought.

'Nothing for it but to cover up all this pain. Take the safe way out. Go back with Peter to where it all began – at the lakeside of Galilee – and go back to fishing.'

Back he went to where his emotional securities lay. Back home.

* * *

Next there was Andrew, Peter's brother. Andrew the optimist.

Every time we read about Andrew he was always saying or doing something positive about his faith. He was the one who brought his brother and his friends to Jesus. He was the one who introduced a Greek tourist party to Jesus after Philip the linguist had done a bit of translation work but was too embarrassed to personally take a bunch of foreigners to Jesus.

At the end of one particularly busy day some months earlier, the rest of the disciples were fed up with the relentless crowds that had pursued them all day and they had said, 'Let's get shot of this lot as soon as possible. It's supper time.' Jesus, however, turned the tables on them and suggested that as his inner circle they might like to feed them. Philip, the realist and sharp with figures, worked it all out and said to Jesus that they'd need at least eight month's wages (combined) to feed that lot.

It was left to Andrew to come up with something positive. Rather naively and a bit over-optimistically he popped his hand up and said, 'I found something. There's a boy over here who's got five rolls and a couple of sardines.' I guess the rest hit their heads with their hands and said, 'Doh.' Some optimists are unbearable in their optimism. With the size of the crowd they'd got that day what was the good of one roll to a thousand men (they typically counted only the men) and a tiddler between two and a half thousand?

'Well, it's a start,' Andrew added with a smile.

And taking those limited resources in his hands Jesus did a miracle.

When we were about to build a large meeting centre for the church family that we had brought together in Luton (and that eventually sent us out to Albania), we had only £10,000 of our own. People thought that we were crazy to think about starting such a large project with so little cash.

My reply to them was, 'If God wants it, we will do it with our own hands – and we will have money enough for all our needs.'

So we started in faith with what we had – a little money and lots of willing people. Before the end of the project, five years later, sufficient money came in to build the whole complex for just under £100,000. (You can read about that exciting story in the earlier book *Bricks Without Straw*.) Wesley, the firebrand of the eighteenth century didn't worry about large human resources. He said, 'Give me ten men who fear nothing but sin and no one but God and I will turn the world upside down.'

For Andrew there was nothing too difficult for Jesus to do. He could cope in any situation, even with this hungry bunch. Jesus justified Andrew's optimism by organising a party, multiplying the boy's lunch, and ending up with twelve large fishing baskets of left-overs after the crowd of at least ten thousand ('five thousand men not counting women and children,' wrote Matthew the accountant) had gone home happily burping on a great fishburger feast. Andrew was an optimist because he had seen Jesus heal the sick. In fact Jesus had miraculously and instantly cured someone in his own home (his brother's mother-in-law who was burning up with a fever). He'd seen Jesus deal with the blind, the deaf, the crippled, the incurables, and he had even seen him give life back to the dead.

Of course Jesus could deal with any difficulty!

But unfortunately now in and after that week that we call 'Holy Week' he didn't.

It was left to Andrew to come up with something positive.

How many times my wife and I have come to a situation full of faith that God would answer prayer, would change peoples lives, would heal the sick, would meet a specific need, and he hasn't. It's a mystery, it's a paradox and it's a pain that we who believe have to live with constantly.

Failure for a *pessimist* isn't a problem. 'Well, I thought it wouldn't work. I knew deep down it wouldn't happen', is their conclusion. Such 'faith-less-ness' obviously gives birth to failure. That is exactly what Jesus said to his followers on the occasion when Andrew, and the other eight who hadn't time to go and pray with Jesus, were left to grapple with their failure and inability to deal with a demonised boy brought to them by his worried dad. 'You can't deal with that sort of thing without faith,' Jesus clearly warned them. But how did Andrew cope now, I wonder, when his *optimism* was shattered like a fragile glass? Failure for an *optimist* is a lot harder to bear.

Sadly a number of 'Faith' Christian groups feel that they have to find an answer to things not happening by putting blame somewhere. So they say the reason for failure and the obstacle to getting things done is 'sin' or 'lack of faith' – generally in the person who has come for help. As a pastor I have had to pick up many already wounded people who have been crushed and trampled into the ground when those two heavy boots have been put in. Christians have to live with a paradox. Jesus who *can*, sometimes *doesn't*. That was the paradox for Andrew. In the end, Jesus the miracle worker let people arrest him, beat him up, and nail him to a cross. For Andrew that was unthinkable.

And there on the cross, like the uncomplaining sheep that people string up by their back legs on a tree or gatepost here in Albania, slit their throats and leave to die, Jesus - the Lamb of God – had died.

What now? Even optimists need a net.

* * *

Finally on the journey up north there were 'two others'.

We aren't told who they were. However, in all probability they were John's older brother James, and his friend Philip. Certainly that would logically complete the Galilee Gang! So, why aren't we told who they were? Maybe it was because they didn't want to be known. There are people who are like that. They like to disappear into the background. They don't want to stand out and be noticed. They don't want people to recognise them. They certainly don't want anyone to make a fuss.

Was James like that? Was Philip like that? James does generally seem to be a tagger-along-er. Although the Bible always talks about 'James and John' (and for this reason I tend to think of James as the older of the two sons of Zebedee) it was always John who made the decisions, or who took the first step. James was there, but always following.

Despite this, Jesus included him in the special triplet that went with him to Jairus' house to bring this church leader's daughter back out from the jaws of death. On another occasion he went with Peter and John up the mountain where Jesus was transformed. There he was privileged to see the divinity of Jesus burst through his humanity brighter than the sun blazing away midday, midsummer. And finally he was allowed to share in the pain of Jesus' last prayer time in the Olive Garden just before Jesus was betrayed by Judas.

But all the while it seems as though James tagged along in the shade, on the edge of the limelight of his more extroverted younger brother. That can happen with brothers and sisters. Maybe it's because with the birth of a second child the first one has to take second place to the new baby's demands and so 'Number 1' gets used to being 'Number 2'.

Only once are we told of an occasion when James did something first. It was just twelve months after the death of Jesus. James was made to literally 'eat (or swallow) his own words' as he was called to drink the cup of suffering that he had so rashly told Jesus a year or so earlier he was ready for. That first Easter anniversary James was summarily murdered by King Herod Agrippa's chief executioner. So James not only died but got to heaven first, fifty years before his younger brother!

Philip, the other possibility, seems to come out in a better light. He at least appears to be someone with a bit of initiative. He brought people to Jesus and he wasn't afraid to ask Jesus questions. But he had his weaknesses and fears as the 'Greek' incident shows.

But then, on the other hand, perhaps I'm trying to be too much of a Sherlock Holmes. Maybe I want everything to be all neat and tidy. And God isn't like that. So I have to say that we really don't know who the other two were. All we know is that they were just there.

And there is a type of person that is just like that. In my ministry I have been so grateful for those 'always there' people. But it's another thing to be private to the point of being secretive. Some people go out of their way to protect themselves with an 'I-don't-want-to-offend-anyone-at any-price' response. Inoffensiveness is good, but not at any price. Then there are those who simply want to hang back in the shadows, unwilling or unable to make decisions.

One of the constant Albanian phrases that we hear just about every day, that is maybe a hangover from the old communist days when personal decisions were discouraged, is something that comes in reply to almost every question which requires a choice. 'Si të duash,' is what people say – which means, 'As you would like.'

Ask anyone to choose in front of a group whether they want a hot or cold drink, coffee or chocolate, a Coke or fizzy water, and in embarrassment they will look at one another, waiting for someone else to make a decision, or whisper frantically to the person next to them, 'What are you having?' If no one ventures to say anything definite that the group can all agree with, the person asked will eventually say, 'Whatever you want. You choose.'

Generally in any group there are at least one or two of those sorts of folk. They are the ones who always go along with the majority, with the people of conviction, with the emphatic ones who are certain about their decisions.

These quiet ones are the *'followers'*. Some followers follow meekly but decisively, but also among the followers there are the 'yes' men and women of society who want to keep the peace at any cost, but who don't realise that it's really not worth trading being true to God or true to themselves just to get a quiet life.

'Followers' not only appreciate a firm hand to guide them but a secure arm to hold them. We all need something like that at some time, but to constantly rely on others leads to an unhealthy dependency. When these folk meet two strong people that they know and respect who hold opposite opinions, they are really confused.

God loves us all as we are, but doesn't want us to stay as we are. He wants us all to ease out of the shadow of others, to stop following them and follow him.

Beside the 'followers' in this group there are what I would call the *'faders'*. In the course of my ministry I have met a number of these shy people. They are the ones who want to melt and mould into the background.

They like big congregations, because they can be lost in the crowd. They like to slip in and out of a service anonymously, and are embarrassed by anything more than a handshake and a simple, 'Nice to see you.'

When, in 1985, we started the new church family in Luton that I mentioned earlier, it began in our home and so it was a very informal sort of church – more of a family. Later on, when we built our own worship place and moved into it we still managed to maintain an informal family atmosphere. In worship we allowed people to be themselves with God. Consequently at any time of worship you might see someone standing with arms stretched up in praise, another clapping, another dancing, while someone else would be sitting quietly worshipping and yet another would be on their knees with hands turned heavenwards. One might be gently laughing, another crying. . . Humanly speaking it was a mess!

More than one person felt uncomfortable with this because, as one of these hesitant people courageously explained to me after yet another of our normally unpredictable services, 'I don't know what to do. There is no model to follow.'

It's amazing how even non-conformists feel secure in conformity.

Because we gave people this 'freedom to be' what they genuinely were in Jesus, a few of the people who attended felt so unsettled that they decided they couldn't continue to come and worship with us.

The lovely thing was that others, just as shy and retiring as them, found security within our freedom to venture out of the shadows a little. Through the total acceptance of the church family they found their sensitivities and perceptions valued, and their thoughts appreciated. They went through a personal pain barrier that did both them and the others in the church good.

But some still needed a crowd. They needed somewhere to hide.

I guess that these two disciples were a bit like that.

* * *

So this happy, or unhappy, motley bunch trekked off to find a bit of normality for their tumultuous lives. Such different personalities – extroverts, introverts, optimists, pessimists, emotionalists, rationalists – all so very different but all carrying the same burden of guilt and failure. This was one thing that despite their differences they all had in common. Each one of them had in fear run away and left Jesus to face the music on his own. They had all blown it. They were all deserters. They could no longer be sure of themselves, and now they felt that they weren't even sure about Jesus. They really were all, literally, in 'the same boat'. Because of their uncertainties each one of them was looking for the same thing – a safety net. Despite being different people with different safety nets they were all experiencing the driving force of the same basic human need - the need for security. Just like us.

Chapter 7

Different Sorts of Nets

Holidays reveal a lot – and I don't just mean on the beaches where human flesh is barbecued in the cause of the 'body beautiful'!

Here are two 'holidays from hell' reports:

Couple 1: It was no holiday. It was a disaster where the tour company put us. We were in the middle of a holiday complex. I couldn't sleep for the constant thump thump thump that pounded in my brain all night from the night club and disco next door. And daytime wasn't much better! The streets swarmed with people in shorts and swimming costumes, jostling one another in order to find a bargain in the shops.

Oh for the peace and quiet of a desert island.

Couple 2: It was no rest. It was awful. I couldn't sleep a wink – it was so quiet. All I heard was the occasional chirp of a cricket. And during the day you could walk for miles (just ONE bus passed through the area and that was only twice a week) and not meet a soul. Just sheep, sheep and more sheep. We were in the middle of nowhere.

Oh for the bright lights, where it's all happening –
where the action is.

We are all so very different. There are those who love to go
somewhere isolated and quiet where they can laze around
and do next to nothing, and then there are those who can't
stand the boredom of seclusion and inactivity. Different
people resort to different means of escape. But what makes
people choose so diversely? Sometimes it's a matter of personality: 'I'm made like that.' Sometimes it's a matter of
upbringing: 'We always went there as kids.' And sometimes it's a matter of culture: 'That's the spot to be. It's the
in place.'

In our village in Albania women can be seen standing
alone or in small groups at their gates – by gate I mean
a six foot solid metal thing that opens out from even
higher walls onto the dusty or, according to the season,
muddy, narrow road. Generally they have a woollen
thread or two hanging round their necks and are knitting with four knitting needles a pair of socks, or a
baby's jacket. As they chat, or as they stand there alone
watching what is going on up and down the road, their
hands are never idle. It's as though they've got to be
doing something.

A busy wife is a good wife is the accepted wisdom.
It's the culturally 'done thing'.

Is that why Albanian women rise at 4.00 a.m. to start
washing the clothes (by hand), baking the bread, cleaning
the footpath from the house to the gate with its front step
going out onto the road, fetching and chopping the wood
for their wood-fired ovens? Later they will have to clean
the house, go out and buy the food, get all the meals,
struggle down the road with large buckets of water from a
nearby pump and all this while their men demand attention – food, coffee, and the lighting of their cigarettes.

A woman's worth is in what she does. That's what every girl learns from her earliest days as she is taught by her mother to clean and tidy up after everyone, and by her brothers (younger or older) to fetch, carry and do whatever the boys demand. That's why parents look for obedient hard-working brides for their sons.

Some people have to keep active because of the *culture*; others have to be active because they are driven by an inner *compulsion*. They can't sit still, they have to do something – it's their security. The saying that controls their lives is, 'The Devil finds work for idle hands, so don't be idle.'

Peter said, 'I'm going fishing. All this emotional up and down from the crucifixion and the resurrection, all this coming and going of Jesus, all this uncertainty about what we should be doing, and all this sitting round inside a bolted and barred flat has phased me. I can't be shut up in a pen. I've got to be out there *doing* something.'

Peter's final resort was always action – verbal or physical. Of course it was also his downfall. He spoke too soon and too often. He acted too quickly and too impetuously. When, at the beginning of his journey of faith, Jesus called him to follow him, without a second thought he downed tools and packed away his net. Later, when John Mark wrote up Peter's story for him (writing never was Peter's strong point – he'd probably skipped school early to get out in someone's fishing boat and I doubt if he ever did his homework), he got Mark to put in the word *'immediately'* when he wrote about how they (Peter and Andrew) left their nets and followed Jesus. In fact Mark's Gospel, which probably reflects a great deal of Peter's personality, is known today as an All Action Book. (Talking about All Action I wonder how Peter's wife and mother-in-law felt about his extrovert,

spontaneously happy-go-lucky, drop-everything, act-
ivist attitude? Maybe Peter should have been called
Big-Foot because he was always jumping into things!)

It was a similar scene up on the mountain where, as
Peter put it, 'We saw the blazing glory of his majestic
divinity.' Without thinking Peter felt he had to fill in one
of those divine silences that come after God speaks.
Peter blurted out the first thing that floated through his
vacuous brain. 'Let's build a Cathedral for all the
tourists on Holy Land Tours to come and visit – in fact
let's build three.'

There are many people who react just like Peter. God's
silences are the times when we are supposed to stop and
think. But what generally happens? If there's a time of
worship and people are asked to be still and listen to
God usually somewhere in the group there is some
Peter-like person who can't stand more than five seconds of quiet and so after a short pause they feel constrained to break out in wavering song, 'Be still and
know that I am God.' They are insecure in what appears
to them to be inactivity. Peter was just like that. His
motto was: When in doubt, don't wait, do something –
something B-I-G!

How many wives of newly retired husbands have
said, as both of them try to adjust to a new and difficult
situation after maybe thirty or more years of daytime
busyness and independence, 'Don't sit there getting
under my feet, do something.' These unsettled wives are
frightened of the Cabbage Syndrome – vegetation –
overtaking their partner. I remember a powerful throw-
away comment by a colleague, who was approaching
imminent retirement, as she said to me in desperation, 'I
don't know what I will do. I don't know how I will cope.
I've got to *do* something.'

Activists are frightened of inactivity.

And it's not just those who are retiring. What is the attraction of the pocket personal stereo/discman that causes young people to sprout black threads from their ears, or worse that makes adolescents lug round on one shoulder an environmentally polluting Ghetto-blaster? Is it the fear of silence, of nothing happening? Maybe it's the daunting prospect of an original thought emerging between those two appendages, where their mini ear-phones plug in or the Blaster explodes through. What would these distracted people do if they started to think or maybe listen to God? What would happen if God got through with an idea that might challenge the media values the music constantly thumps in – values that they subtly imbibe and feel they have to slavishly follow?

Maybe that is why, in fact, the Devil *does* find work for idle hands and minds. He can't stand stillness, in case God gets through.

When things are uncertain, or on the other hand as an answer to or a penance for messing things up, some people just *have* to do something, whatever it may be, to compensate. That compensatory action can mean any-thing from kicking the cat or taking the dog for a brisk walk; bingeing on a large bar of chocolate or getting hopelessly stoned; through to the escapism of running away or blowing their brains out.

Rather than reflect these people react.

Their net is activity.

* * *

Similar to activism, but for a different reason, is work.

They're similar because they are both about things we do, and in turn what we can be 'driven' by. But then they are different. Activism is nebulous, anything will do to fill up our time or act as a distraction, whereas work is specific. Work has value, at it we produce things, and it gives us personal good feelings of achievement. It has kudos as it is recognised, is related to ability, and so gets approval from others. And it has profit – it gets us money.

Peter chose not just to do something – any old thing – but to go back fishing. Fishing was his work, his life, his everything before meeting Jesus. So like a homing pigeon he returned to his former security, his job. Fishing was what he'd been a success at before his new start with Jesus – something which had resulted in his recent and terrible 'failure'.

Many peoples' net in difficulty, uncertainty, or failure is their work. It's the place where they fill their troubled minds with legitimate distractions. It's the place where they find not only fulfilment but also their self-assurance. They are confident, they are secure, when they are doing their work. Though, often as not, they are driven by it. In addition, significance for many people is found in what is called 'job satisfaction' and value and meaning too are frequently rooted in achievement. Generally this stems from a person's childhood, and though not genetically inherited is generally inculcated at an early age by perfectionist parents in collusion with educational establishments.

My wife started a small school exclusively for girls in our village of Bregu-i-Lumit after a number of parents asked for one. It met in the church that we started on the second floor of our house. Quite justifiably these parents had been apprehensive about allowing their teenage daughters to travel into the capital on the local bus for secondary schooling. They had withdrawn them from the state system because of a fear that the girls might be kidnapped and sold off into prostitution in Italy and Greece. We knew of at least five youngsters that this had happened to in our first four years there. In fact one was from our school, though she was abducted later in the day when she was at someone else's house. Parental desire for protection for their daughters overrode their strong desire for educational excellence. So they were well pleased to have a school just round the corner.

Anyway, every year my wife, Heather, held an 'open day' for parents and friends to come and see the students' work. Most times she has had to explain about the marks she has given to the girls, that these were based on the more objective British percentage system. In the Albanian marking system parents always expect ten out of ten for everything, and are so disappointed and even angry when their daughters don't get it. Sadly in many cases an Albanian 'ten' can mean anything from 'Perfect' and 'Well done', through 'That's what I usually give you' or 'I like you', to 'That's what you get if you give me a backhander.' Many are the times when distraught children have returned home from State school with an arbitrary eight out of ten – despite hard work – simply because the teacher hasn't looked at their work properly. There is a deep sense of injustice and despair among the students when those with ten out of ten turn out to be the ones whose parents have paid the teacher to give good results in order to get their child into university. So often we have heard disheartened youngsters saying to one another, 'It's not fair, my work was better than theirs!' And it's true!

Unfortunately the problem is then compounded when many of the children who have failed to gain the expected ten out of ten through no fault of their own are subsequently called 'failures' by their parents. They are shouted at, and sometimes physically beaten. No wonder perfectionism has such a powerful control in Albania and people are 'driven' by the compulsion to be achievers. They are devastated by failure.

Generally lurking somewhere in the shadows that surround the harsh unyielding light of perfectionism we can find the ogre of fear. The person who first said, 'Comparisons are odious' must have known something about the foul smell of fear.

And sadly we all do it – compare that is! Competition isn't bad, it gives incentive – that's why school sports days are good. But the rod of comparison that leads to judgmentalism and belittlement is not good. It's not good for two reasons. On the one hand comparison feeds fear in those who land on their faces at the bottom of the rugby scrum of comparison, and on the other hand fosters pride in those who come out on top with the ball.

Even at clergy gatherings I have heard this principle at work – except it is put very subtly by those who are more successful. After the usual 'How are you?' comes the question 'And how are things?' With an air of disappointment and dubious humility the questioner goes on to say: 'Not a good day yesterday, we only had just under five hundred at the service', or 'A great day yesterday, but only twelve baptised this time.' The rest of us who are listening in, with feelings of abject failure, wonder if we will ever even begin to get into triple figures, let alone achieve half of a four-figure congregation!

How envious and guilty the majority feels when the successful man talks about his fourth full-time fully paid member of staff. Most of the group are struggling not only to keep the evening service going, but generally have a wife who acts as pianist, junior church leader, as well as both husband and wife having to act as church caretakers, cleaners and repairers.

And yet. . .

Look below the surface of the confidently smiling 'successful' person and often there can be seen a shadowy inner figure who is biting his fingernails, frantically studying stat charts and judging his worth by his work.

Even those of us working for God overseas (we who are called 'missionaries'), when writing back to base and our supporting churches, have to watch out for that twin-peaked iceberg which, like the one that sank the Titanic, brings disaster to many a serving vessel. On the one side there is the dangerous peak of 'overemphasising' our successes and on the other side the peak of 'under-stating' or even 'side-stepping' our failures. Folks 'back home' want to read how *great* we are doing. Some of them can't understand that 'missionaries' have personal difficulties, let alone suffer from a depression like the one I experienced.

Three missionaries are having problems with one another, but some people don't want to hear about failures

I will never forget one missionary meeting held in a church in the UK that I was in charge of in the early days of my ministry. We were divided up into discussion groups by the missionary who was taking the event, and each group was given a problem to work through. In my group the question we were given to discuss was something along the lines of the following: 'There are three missionaries living and working together in a remote village six days travel away from any other missionaries. They are having problems getting on with one another. What can be done to help them sort out their situation?' One dear soul looked at me in amazement with mouth agog and said with a stutter, 'B-b-b-but pastor, they are missionaries!' as though that were an antidote to differences and difficulties. Maybe she thought that missionaries live on another planet.

Some people simply don't want to hear about failures and, what is worse, they don't want to pray for or financially support those who don't come up with the goods. That sort of attitude puts tremendous pressures on Christian workers to be 'successful'. It stirs up in them the 'I've-got-to-achieve-at-all-costs-or-I-won't-be-supported' mentality. Sidling up to that attitude comes the thought that 'I've got to show people that I am a perfect saint or I will be letting the side down.' That in turn leads to a 'My-worth-is-in-my-work' mind-set and finally creates the 'My-security-is-in-my-work' safety net.

* * *

Some have security in what they do, others in *who* they do it with.

When Peter said, 'I'm going fishing,' the other six said, 'Don't leave us on our own. We have to stick together. Solidarity in numbers, brothers. Security in togetherness.'

Better for failures to stick together.

Better to fall together than to fall alone.

When my daughters were very small and at their first school they came home with a rhyme that they had learned in the playground, 'Make friends, Make friends,

Never never break friends. If you do, you'll catch the flu, and that will be the end of you.' In the light of that threat it's amazing how many friendships were made, broken, remade, ruptured and then repaired – and all without 'flu' or 'death'! More amazing is the sad fact that out of those many bold but fragile relationships started in school only one or two have stood the test of time and continued into adulthood.

A friendship that lasts and is unconditional is a rare find.

At a Serendipity conference that I went to in the eighties we were asked the question, 'Do you have a friend that you can call up at any hour of the day or night and know that they won't mind, and who you know will want to help you?'At the time I thought that I had one. Sadly, some months later when I really needed him he turned his back on me with a judgmental attitude, and I've not heard a dicky bird from him since.

Despite the risk of rejection, it's to our friends we turn when things go wrong. 'A problem shared is a problem halved,' we are told. To which we could add: Broken hearts need people. Way back in the beginning when God's hands were still drying off from the damp clay from which he made the first man, Adam, and just as he, the perfect Creator, was about to put his 'seal of approval' sticker on this peak of his creation, we read how God stopped and pronounced his first ever 'Not good' statement.

'It's not good for this one to be on his own,' he said, 'he needs a friend.' And looking round at all the creatures he had made he added, 'He needs a human companion.'

So God came up with the idea of a woman that the man could share his ups and downs with. At the same time the man in his turn could be a shoulder for her to lean on. In fact God decided that they could both be a mutual help to each other. Eve was the prototype of caring. She was the perfect model of someone who would meet the basic need of every human being for friendship. And everyone, ever since, has found it necessary at some time to have a friend. Even Jesus

I'm fascinated, and at times amazed, when I think about Jesus, that he not only chose to tramp around Palestine with a really rough bunch of blokes, sharing life and eternity with them, but that at the end of his journey he chose to depend on three of them at his darkest moment. That last night in Olive Trees Garden, when facing a life and death issue Jesus asked his closest friends, Peter, James and John, to stick by him and pray along with him. Three weak men, who fell asleep on the job not just once but *three* times, were asked to shoulder the burden of Jesus' agonising choice as to whether to choose death on a cross for all the mistakes and wrongs of the world or to take the easy road and fly straight back to the peace and quiet of heaven. Did he *really* need them?

Amazingly, from what Jesus said, the answer was 'Yes'. That's why it hurt so much when they let him down in that lonely place of prayer and then later when, as the troops came to arrest him, they made a bolt for it. It hurt Jesus when in the end they left him to die alone. The truly divine, completely human, Jesus turned to his friends for support just like we do.

But, unlike us, people weren't his ultimate security.

* * *

Then there are those who when troubles or pressures come, or when failure happens, have a bolthole to which they can run and hide. *Escapism* is their safety net.

Peter basically said, 'I'm off, whatever you lot decide to do.'

We once owned an Alsatian bitch that my parents rescued from someone's outhouse. She was bought by them to be the companion of Saturn Prince, a pedigree Alsatian dog that we had, in the hope that they would produce a litter of beautiful, quality pups. She did well and gave us a litter of twelve, one of which was a perfect white puppy with a black nose and deep golden eyes.

But when we first brought this pathetic creature home she had hardly any fur on her haunches due to being locked up most of her life in a shed, and she constantly flinched due to being beaten with sticks. As soon as we released her into our large back garden she skulked in fear around the dark unknown edges until she saw the kennel that my Dad had made for her and in blind panic she made a beeline for it. There she cowered with terror in her eyes. When I crept in to stroke her and comfort her she crouched at the back of the kennel shaking and trembling, and started to snarl with fear thinking I was going to hit her. She would constantly pull away into the furthest corner trying to hide in the darkness.

It took months of patient work to ease her out of her seclusion, and many more before we were eventually able to see her frisking round the garden with her mate. But it only needed one unexpected sound, or a shout, and she'd be back in the dark recesses of her kennel like a shot.

Her security was retreat and seclusion.

Elijah was a bit like that. After the somewhat unfair contest on the top of a mountain (450 to 1) when he called down fire from heaven (like James and John wanted to) to ignite a sacrifice on the altar of the Lord that he had prepared and soaked with gallons of sea water and God answered his call; and following the time immediately afterwards when he prayed and called down rain after a three-and-a-half-year drought and again God did a miracle; poor Elijah suffered from what today would be called 'burnout'. Like our frightened dog he suddenly disappeared off into the back of beyond, up on another mountain, and went and hid in the back of a cave with a tear-stained face moaning, 'I've failed. I'm the only one left who wants to serve the Lord. I want to die.' Is that how Peter felt? Did he just want to get away from everything and everyone? Did he simply want to escape?

There are people who feel the same today.

Many Albanians, after 1997 and the ensuing period of anarchy when the country fell apart, after the loss of money and jobs, after the loss of members of their family through 'revenge killings' (that once started can continue until all the men of the two opposed groups are wiped out), and after the loss of hope for the future, lots of them said to us, 'I just don't want to live. I want to die.'

My mother, after my father suffered a prolonged heart illness called bacterial endocarditis, plus stress in the church that she had been looking after in his absence, plus pressures in the insurance business my parents owned, plus the delights of a teenage son flexing his muscles, subsequently had a nervous breakdown and became suicidal. She wanted out – to end her life; to hide from her feelings of inadequacy and failure; to escape all the problems.

And now I understand her. Six months after the death of our youngest daughter I slipped into what the doctors called a reactive depression. On one or two occasions as I walked alone along the beach where my wife and I were staying the sea seemed very magnetic and enticing. To swim, and swim, and swim . . . into the oblivion of death where there was no more pain, confusion or darkness. That escape route from the blackness I was in looked very welcoming . . . until my brain kicked into gear and told me that the rest of my family had suffered just as much as me and would suffer much greater pain if anything happened to me as well.

But that was the sort of 'flight' reaction that happened to people in the Bible just as much as it happened to me. Even young David, the one who was called a 'delight to the Lord', in one of his very personal songs in that Bible songbook called Psalms, wrote: 'O to have wings, wings to fly away.' And both Job and Jeremiah felt the same. They said that the oblivion of death was a very attractive option in the midst of all they were going through. How inviting at times that 'opt out' clause can appear to us – just to be able to escape all the pain that we are going through and to be free of it all.

Pain of course can have a positive purpose in our lives – it's there to tell us that something is wrong – but pain in itself can also be a great hindrance to progress. One day an elderly but spritely lady who attended one of my churches stood on some canes that she had bought to support her runner beans. She skidded on them, fell, and broke her hip. After a somewhat lengthy stay in hospital and a convalescent home she returned to her own flat, but she became a self-imposed prisoner there. She was afraid to put too much pressure on the now fully healed hip 'in case it might give way', she would say. So out of fear she locked herself away in the security of her own little home.

Over the years it has been my privilege from time to time to visit some of the members of my different churches in special hospitals that care for the troubled, disturbed and sick in mind. How sad it was to see in one of those institutions a large room full of patients, row upon row of them just sitting there. Some who had shut out the harsh world of reality and retreated into a comfortable world of their own, and others who were helped with sedatives to shut out the nightmares that had become daily living realities.

That's an extreme form of escapism. Less dramatic and drastic, but just as problematical, is the situation of the person who, for one reason or another, drops out of society in order to sleep on the streets. These people, often called 'drop-outs', congregate along the London Embankment, and in other similar places in most large cities. They range from those who've never held down a job for more than a few weeks through to professional people who can't face the pressures of work and home anymore; kids who have been abused and who end up abusing themselves with drugs; people who have hit financial problems through unemployment or some failing to qualify for the benefits that others take for granted; as well as those to whom society has given a rough deal and doesn't seem to care. Life for all of them has become unbearable: a kaleidoscope of pain. Huddled under their cardboard shelters there are many individ-uals seeking anonymity and the safety of non-entity.

Escape.

As Shakespeare put it, 'To sleep, to rest, and then perchance to dream. . .'

When I went through some troubled times as a pastor of a church in the UK and felt that I couldn't take much more pressure and criticism, I used to come home, at times struggling to hold back the tears, and would say to my wife, 'I'm going to be a dustman.' My dream was to be a carefree refuse collector. That seemed to me to be the most inviting thing to do to get out of the snares and cares of my overbearing responsibilities. That would be my escape – at least it was in my mind, as I never actually did it.

* * *

Finally there are the 'There's no place like home' folks.

The aura of the familiar is coloured a warm attractive pink.

How many couples experiencing marital dullness or difficulties have lived to regret the day when they thought it would be a good idea to return to that idyllic honeymoon spot in an attempt to recapture the past and found it to be as disappointing as their present relationship. The beauty of the place has rarely been the location but the love that caused the sunset to blush, the moon to glow with reflected joy and the stars to twinkle at the fun shared by two love-intoxicated hearts.

After ten years of marriage my wife and I thought it would be fun to show our two daughters where we spent our honeymoon and have lunch at the same hotel. Disaster.

We looked with sadness at the faded tablecloths and jaded furniture. Even the table lamps seemed to be bent with age. It was a good job that we had only come out of curiosity and not to recapture something we had lost.

The ultimate weapon that is often used in a crumbling relationship is summed up in the well-worn statement, 'I'm going home to mother.' Isn't that where we all used to run when bruised from a fall, ridiculed or bullied at school, or when the boyfriend or girlfriend said that they had found someone better?

We all have a homing instinct stronger than a pigeon.

So Peter and his friends, under pressure, surrounded by uncertainties, and plagued with guilt went back up north. Back home. Back to the familiar sights, smells and sounds. The lulling rocking rhythm on Galilee Lake of the waves lapping against the gunnels. The bracing wind whipping against them to burnish their crest-fallen faces that once glowed with satisfaction. The long forgotten smell of slimy fish flapping in the bottom of the boat. Home cooking, the aroma of fresh hot bread, and the old familiar creaking bed. Home, sweet home.

When there is no place to go to in difficulties it's to the safety of home that we run.

It's amazing how powerful and attractive the familiar is when we look for security. In one of my churches there was a lady in her nineties who sat three rows from the front, down on my right, surrounded by empty wooden pews. Like in most churches the majority of the other people loved to congregate at the back. We even had a gallery that some members preferred. During the first days of my ministry in that place you would have been hard pressed to fly a paper dart from one attender to another.

We closed the gallery and encouraged everyone to come downstairs and closer to the front in the middle, but this dear lady remained steadfastly attached to her seat as though glued there. When I asked her why she sat there in such splendid isolation, she replied, 'I was brought into this family pew by my parents as a baby, I've sat here all my life, and I'll die here' – something that I was frightened that one Sunday she might actu-ally do!

There is a security in the familiar.

Why is it that many of the elderly are heard to say, 'Fings ain't what they used to be'?

Was life really that much better? Did the sun always shine on holiday? Did people seriously always care that much more? Were folk really that much more moral? Maybe it's because, with hindsight, the things of the past have become somewhat blurred due to the time that has elapsed since people went through them.

The past is secure because it is past. It's the future, all unknown, that is frightening.

Over the years, in church life, this underlying issue of security that's found in the familiar and in the past has expressed itself in many ways, but nowhere more than in worship. My, the battles that have raged over the eruption of new songs and different forms of worship! Okay. Some new things have been mere fads. Some are merely 'imports' and cheap reproductions of genuine inspirations from God elsewhere – as though copying means spirituality. I can still see in my mind a young man at a Christian celebration looking round and watching hands being raised in praise. Gradually, as he became a minority, he lifted his own hands to half mast while continuing to gaze around with confusion on his face as he tried to get into what the others were obviously enjoying.

Let's be honest, there are things about worship that are at times more people-centred than God-centred, and certainly there are a number of people who are more concerned about what 'pleases me' than what might 'please God'. Some people are never content without getting the latest novelty, gizmo, or following the newest fad.

But on the other hand . . . I ask the question: why do people fight so hard against the new? Basically because, beside there being some genuine criticisms of banal worship, there is a type of Christian whose security has been, and humanly speaking always will be, in the old and familiar. I'm grateful for a wife who on many occasions has reminded me that the inability to be flexible and to change is a sign of old age. Unfortunately there are lots of 'old people' around (and not all of them are old in years either) who equate loyalty with what is called 'our spiritual heritage' (which in fact is nothing more than conformity to their own secure pattern) as a sign of spiritual maturity. Yes, there are basic things that we must hold firmly to, 'the faith once delivered to the saints', but if we are really honest, as often as not those basics are a lot less in number than we are comfortable to admit. Maturity is the ability to recognise what is foundational to our faith – that is what God has said and done – while at the same time being able to see what God is doing and where he is leading. Maturity is the ability to remember the benefits of the past and step out into the new. We are told many times in the Bible that here on earth we have no eternal securities. Here we are pilgrims on the move, stepping forward into what the Lord has prepared – the yet to be. But some hands can't hold on to the foundations of the past and some feet can't move into the promise of the future.

The inability to move confidently forward into the new while holding on to the old says more about spiritually arthritic joints than a strong mature faith. My daily prayer is, 'God, I don't want to be an old man who loses it on the last lap.'

When everything seems to be changing and other Christians seem to be discovering and expressing their love for God in what appears to be a rash flush of real love – well, that sort of thing is threatening to any insecure, rigid, or duty-bound heart. Such insecure church people prefer the safety of 'nostalgic' rather than 'prophetic' worship, the 'familiarly recognised' to the 'unknown'.

It's the same retreat mentality that causes us to turn to other well-worn securities. How many fishermen or gardeners have discovered at a jumble sale what their wives have cleared out in a spring clean. Triumphantly they have bought back their battered old hats or boots. 'It would be like losing an old friend,' has been their retort to a disgusted wife.

* * *

For some, or maybe all, of these reasons the Galilee Fishermen's Fraternity went back up north searching for safety in uncertainty, and a way out of their troubles.

Chapter 8

Unexpected Encounters

We've all had them at some time or other – unexpected encounters.

First there is the, 'Well, you were the last person I expected to see here' reaction, and then there's the, 'I hardly recognised you' comment.

On one occasion we were leaving Albania for a short visit, going back to see our family in England. There we were in Albania's International Airport chatting to a young American man when a lady I was supposed to have talked to on the phone about some relief food, and had been unable to contact, came into the waiting room.

'Fancy meeting you here,' we said to one another, and in a matter of half an hour, while waiting for our respective planes – hers to Holland and ours to Heathrow – we were able to sort out the basics for a plan to feed a number of hungry children in our village.

On another occasion I was at a meeting in the UK, and was being stared at by a young lady – an unusual thing for me at my age! Then the penny dropped. She was someone my wife and I had met years ago. To stop her perplexity I went over and spoke to her. 'Yes, it is Ryder

Rogers, and I've grown a beard for a drama in our church and because I'm now a grandfather.'

Unexpected encounters. Unexpected appearances.

A bit like Jesus.

Throughout his life, Jesus not only turned up at some most unexpected moments, but at times he appeared in most unexpected ways. You wouldn't reckon on meeting him in the pitch black of the early hours of the morning, mid-channel, crossing from one side of an inland choppy sea to the other. Not when you are in a boat and he is happily skipping from one wave to the next on top of the water. However, if you were a regular card-carrying church member and attender you wouldn't be at all surprised to see Jesus standing in the front row of the local congregation where the keenest and most important of them assembled.

But then if you were a member of one of the narrower-minded church cliques who were generally to be found sitting there at the front of the church in all their glory, you certainly wouldn't expect to see the 'Holy One of Israel' next door with some of those unsavoury neighbours. Most definitely you couldn't in your wildest dreams imagine him at a private bottle party packed with shady characters who fiddled the books. No way could you think of him surrounded by highly made-up women of a distinctly scarlet shade.

No wonder Jesus got the names 'sinner sympathiser' and 'alcohol abuser' from the church of his day. And it didn't help his case when he smiled with delight at these 'holier-than-thou' people's criticisms with the reply that that's why he had come from heaven – to be 'The Failure's Friend'.

You don't expect that sort of thing from the Son of God.

And you couldn't ever think of finding him sitting on the edge of a well in the full blaze of the midday sun chatting away about spiritual matters not only with a despised foreigner whose people had warped your religion into a charade, but a man-eater who had got through five husbands and was living with her next victim.

Jesus was so. . . well. . . 'inconsistent'. Well, that would be the opinion of those sort of people who only saw life in glaring 'black and white'. His life was full of so many unsettling paradoxes. But that is Jesus.

He seemed to be as much at ease in the home of a church leader like Jairus as he was in the home of a social reject like Zacchaeus. He was just as happy to talk all night to one of the leaders of the Jewish synod called Nicodemus as to spend time with a 'madman', possessed by an army of evil spirits, calling himself 'Legion'. His feet straddled both camps.

The only people he couldn't stand were hypocrites. To the Jewish religious leaders of the day who hung around the edges of the crowds waiting to hear something that they could trap Jesus with, Jesus said, 'You bunch of hypocrites, looking so clean on the outside, but being like a stained coffee cup on the inside! You're all show. You are stumbling blocks to the blind. You don't help anyone find God, in fact you make things more difficult for those who are really seeking the truth. You are like snakes in the grass. You are a poison and a danger to all around!'

And Jesus was no less direct with Christians in the book of Revelation. When speaking to the churches in Turkey, and specifically to a congregation in a city called Laodicea, he said, 'You hypocrites make me want to spit.'

'You are just like the tepid water that bubbles up from your natural springs. Spring water that is neither thirst-quenching nor palatable. I'd be happier if you froze me out like ice-cold water than to have you just lukewarm. Though actually, I'd prefer you to be steaming hot.' Bluntly he concluded his message by saying, ' Laodicea, at times you make me want to throw up.'

Isn't that shocking? At times God isn't even polite! We certainly don't expect that sort of thing from 'gentle Jesus, meek and mild'! But then that's not how he really is. The Jesus of the Bible says and does the most unexpected things.

After his death, the risen and truly alive Jesus turned up in the strangest of places and some most unusual ways. His first appearance was in the Garden of Remembrance *outside* his burial cave, not inside. He next appeared suddenly in a heavily locked room where all his followers were hiding from the secret police thinking it was their turn next. Then he was seen casually wandering along a village road when all devout Jews were returning home after evening worship. And now here he was cooking breakfast by the beach as the runaways were facing more failure after a night of pointless fishing.

But it wasn't just the occasions when, and places where, he appeared. At times it was his actual appearance that was strange. There are fascinating and perplexing clues about these unusual appearances that can take up hours of thought and give us plenty to chew over.

For example, what about Jesus' first appearance – to Mary? Okay, as I said earlier, her bloodshot eyes, through lack of sleep and tears, probably didn't help. But why after two or three years of following Jesus, day in, day out, didn't she recognise either his looks or his voice? It wasn't until after she had impetuously said that she'd take away the body of Jesus single-handed and he, in reply, gave her that smiling word of incredulity, 'Oh Mary!', that the penny dropped. Only then did she fall on her knees to kiss his feet.

Yet even then, in that moment when she tried to embrace him, Jesus said a strange thing as he drew back from her. There is deep mystery in his statement. 'Don't touch me. I haven't shown myself to my Father in heaven yet.' Strange, because later on, in fact on that same day at his evening meeting with the eleven, he said exactly the opposite. 'Feel my hands,' he told them, 'Ghosts don't have skin and bones like me.'

What happened in those few hours of daylight that changed his orders from 'Don't touch' into 'Feel me'? Something changed. In the first incident, the one at the graveside with Mary, had the mortal not yet fully put on immortality? Was Jesus so different in the garden that we have to say that when this human body puts on the heavenly and we are changed that we are actually *changed* somehow?

But then once again, I sometimes wonder what it was that was so unrecognisable about Jesus when he was travelling down the road from Jerusalem to Emmaus. What was it that stopped Cleopas and his wife seeing it was Jesus as he walked shoulder to shoulder with them for nearly two hours on their five-mile journey home? Was it just their heated discussion and their arguing that blinded them (as arguments invariably do to anyone and anything outside our already firmly set pre-conceptions)?

I struggle with the question: Why didn't they know it was Jesus? After all, Cleopas's wife was there at the cross with Mary and the other women only a day or so earlier. Was it all just a matter of their ideas being fixed, and an example of how the 'closed-mind syndrome' kept them, as it keeps us, from recognising him? Or was there something else?

Luke definitely says that there was 'something' that stopped them.

And then I ask, what does Mark really mean when he says about this incident in such clear language, 'And Jesus appeared in another guise'?

Does Peter's own private experience of Jesus have anything to add to this? It's an event that is passed over in a matter of a few words (though it was later confirmed by Paul in one of his letters). Dr Luke writes down words from the lips of one of the eleven, 'The Lord has risen and been seen by Peter.'

Then we have to add to the evidence this early morning encounter with Jesus by the lakeside. We *could* excuse the failure of Peter and his friends to recognise Jesus by Galilee Lake in all sorts of ways. After all, it was before sunrise. The light wasn't good. They were a bit far off from the shore, etc. But, I ask myself, was that all? Is this account giving us yet further information for the self-same mystery of the unrecognised and unexpected Jesus?

Did Jesus have a different facial and bodily appearance after his resurrection?

After death did he in fact look so battle-scarred that he now appeared to Mary like a weather-worn gard-ener? Isaiah did say something about the battered features of the sacrificial Lamb of God, 'There's nothing handsome or attractive about him', in fact some people 'hide their faces from him'.

Did Jesus really look so different? Did he look like a stranger to the two travellers on Emmaus Road as he did to others who were his followers?

Was his appearance only different in their own eyes or was it possible for Jesus to actually alter his appearance to take people by surprise?

Our God is a God of surprises. This is evident in the first part of the Bible, which we call the Old Testament. Abraham one day invited three unknown tourists to be his guests and to share lunch with him. Later on in the day he discovered that it was the Lord God himself accompanied by two of his archangels – all three of them looking like ordinary travellers. That was some surprise.

If, as the writer to Jewish believers says, 'some can unexpectedly and unknowingly meet and give hospitality to angels' can we not meet the Lord in unexpected ways and forms? I don't mean in some syncretistic way as the root of all being, in the beauty of his creation, or in some mystic way meeting him in others (which are really only the reflection not the substance of the Lord). I mean meeting *him*.

I often think about Moses. There he was happily minding his own business looking after some sheep in the back of beyond. The dry and dusty land of Midian was the place where he had ended up as a refugee after failing to help his own people who were slaves to the Pharaoh-King. After killing an Egyptian officer in an abortive attempt to free the people of God in his own way, he ran away into the scrub-land of Midian to learn God's way. Suddenly, one day while he was minding his new father-in-law's sheep, his eye was caught by a scraggy bush that seemed to have ignited itself by self-combustion in the scorching heat, but mysteriously wasn't burning up.

As he got nearer to have a look at this curious sight, he was stopped in his tracks by a voice that called him personally by name and told him to take his shoes off and get down on his knees because he was in the presence of the God of all creation. Unsought, and un-expected, this man who tried to do something for God in his own strength and failed, had a surprise encounter with the Lord who would show him *his* power and plan.

This was a God he was so surprised to meet that he had to ask, 'Excuse me, what is your name?'

I've mentioned the 'unexpected encounter' I had in the ruins of Fountains Abbey in Yorkshire, but that wasn't the only time.

How many of us treat the evangelical obligation of 'the Quiet Time' (a daily time for Bible reading and prayer) with an almost Pharisaical legalism. We do it, as often as not, because we were told to when we first became Christians and now because we feel we ought to. But if we are honest, as often as not, we do it as a duty, mixed with a dose of fear, and that prevents us from expecting much to happen that's good.

Don't get me wrong. I'm all for a time, or more than one, set aside for the Lord each day – this book sprang out of that! It's the fear of failure that many people live under for not doing it regularly or long enough that I'm against. It's the oppressive and misguided thought that if we miss our God-slot God might come down and blast us to smithereens for a missed appointment. God isn't an employer who will dismiss us for not turning up for work, or an army officer who will throw us in jail for being AWOL. He is a father who is waiting with gifts, a mother waiting with hugs, a lover waiting with kisses. It's not that we will be judged, but that we might miss out.

A bit like Thomas on Easter Sunday. Where was he, I wonder? All the others were locked in their upstairs room together. Had he stayed too long elsewhere when curfew came? Was he just not interested? Was he too bound up in personal grief? Had he simply given up? What sense of failure burned in him and stopped him from being there? Whatever the cause, the consequence was that he missed the first public appearance of Jesus to his special friends.

It's not what God might do *against* us that's the frightening thing for absentees, it's what he might do *without us* that we could miss out on – that's the worrying thing!

Anyway, this time I was at my aunt's council flat in south-east London for a visit. I was feeling that I might end up like disappointed Thomas as I was missing out on some special and exciting meetings at the church I was attending during my sabbatical in 1982. Every so often my mind drifted from the conversation she and my mother were having about family, holidays, the state of the nation, etc., to what was possibly happening at the church.

After some toast all soggy with butter (my aunt had a beautifully cuddly figure because she loved lots of real butter) and a night-cap of hot chocolate, then hugs all round before traipsing off to the bathroom for a quick wash, I finally got into my bedroom for a short read of my Bible and a quick 'good-night' prayer before tucking down for the night.

My passage for the day was Psalm 116. In David's song I was particularly drawn to focus on verses 12 and 13: 'What can I give to the Lord for all the good things he has done for me? I will accept the cup of salvation and call on the name of the Lord.' As I thought about, and admitted, my own emptiness and my inability to do anything except to receive, a strange quiet came over me as I waited, thirsty for a drink from that heavenly cup.

Suddenly, and unexpectedly, it was as though a fire fell and burned right through me. As a good Bible-believing Christian I quickly said, in a bit of a panic, 'If this is of the Devil, I rebuke it. I put myself under the protection of the blood of Jesus. Jesus is Lord.' Then breaking through my apprehension I became aware of a quiet voice that said simply, 'It's me.'

It was the Lord, catching me out in my daily quiet time, meeting me, speaking to me, and filling me with his Spirit.

That time with Jesus, which I thought was going to be a quick prayer before a long sleep, became an unexpected hour or two of undiluted pleasure in the company of the Lord Jesus.

I suppose that it was a bit like that for Peter, James and John up the mountain. Jesus said, 'Who's for prayer?' Typically 75 per cent of the church wasn't interested in a prayer meeting. But they were the losers because there in prayer Jesus was transformed – 'metamorphosed' is the actual word, which literally means 'physically changed'.

There it is again: 'appearing in a different form'. On that special occasion on Metamorphosis Mountain a divine glory shone through the transparency of Jesus' human flesh as his face shone brighter than the midday sun and his clothes whiter than any ancient or modern biological powder could possibly make them. When he recalled this event later, Peter wrote, 'We saw his majesty.'

Then there was the time I've mentioned before when the disciples were surprised by the unrecognised Jesus as they were crossing the lake one evening and got caught in a storm that kept them all night rowing head on into the waves to prevent them from capsizing. They were making no progress at all. Suddenly in the middle of the lake an eerie figure approached and was just on the point of passing them by. Something unusual like that made them think that it must a ghost. But it turned out to be Jesus.

Jesus unexpectedly meets us not only in broad daylight, and on the tops of prayer mountains, but in the middle of the night on stormy waters when we feel we're about to drown. He is always there just when we need him, but not always as we expect him.

During our evacuation process when we had to leave Albania, one of our team at Albania's main port was hit in the back of the head by a ricochet bullet. Most of us were waiting in the grounds of the British Embassy in the capital, Tirana, to form a convoy to go to the same port when, on our two-way missionary radios, one of our party heard the message, 'Debbie's been shot.' Debbie and her husband had travelled the day before with their children in their mini-bus to the port of Durres to catch a ferry to Italy. The ferry had almost arrived when it backed away due to all the gunfire and left the waiting passengers on the quay. After the boat had backed off, and they were left waiting on the quay-side, suddenly a stray bullet slammed against Debbie's skull and knocked her to the ground.

A vehicle was quickly found for her and she was put inside. But what were they to do now? How could they safely get to the hospital with all the shooting and loot-ing going on? Unexpectedly a tall Albanian appeared through the crowd of onlookers, got into the vehicle with them and took them by a circuitous, deserted and totally unknown route to the hospital. When they turned round to thank him, in the large and empty open space outside the hospital where they had stopped, he had simply just disappeared. Debbie and her husband are certain that it was an angel that the Lord sent to guide and protect them.

Sporting a large white compress she later returned to the port and was among the first foreigners to be res-cued by the Italian Navy. However her husband and fourteen-year-old daughter weren't so lucky and were forced with the rest of us 'non-Italians' to endure a night that included being dazed by Italian stun grenades and shot at by the mariners as they left the port with two empty landing craft. We had to face the threats of the angry and confused Albanians who now surrounded us. We also had to survive the feeling of abandonment and uncertainty as the darkest part of the night swirled round our heads and hearts.

It wasn't just the darkness of the night and the bewilderment of stun grenades that was swirling around my heart. It was the increasing feeling of devastation that we were escaping and failing our dear brothers and sisters, leaving them alone to face the discordant music of anarchy. And yet, paradoxically, in all the confusion of our human feelings there was a sort of peace, even a sense of wonder. As I looked up I saw for the first time in the starry black night sky the clear outline of the comet, complete with its dusty tail, that everyone had been talking about on the news.

Where did that peace come from? Yes, the verse came to mind, 'The heavens declare the glory of God.' With this verse came the thought that he who holds on to the stars with all their boundless and explosive energies, was holding all us fugitives and this land writhing in the agony of anarchy. But there was something more to it than that. The next day, or the day after (those traumatic hours somehow all blurred into one), we found out what it was. In the tranquillity of our daughter's house Heather and I read the passage from Isaiah that was recommended by our *Encounter with God* Scripture Union notes for the day that covered the midnight hour that we had spent waiting at our Albanian port of departure. In our Albanian Bible one verse boldly stood out that translates, 'I am the Lord. I have put my arms around you to surround you.' Yes, the Lord was there with us, with all his heavenly commandoes.

Many hours and miles later after our evacuation from the Albanian port of Durres, as we cruised high up in the sky in a BA jet that the British Government had chartered to take us from Italy back to the UK, and as we were about to eat our first meal for thirty-three hours, one of the Irish nuns who had been evacuated along with us led us in a prayer of thanks over the plane's PA system. She thanked the good Lord for his care for us, and for his angels who had been with us and around us throughout this difficult experience.

Even the atheists who had been with us gave a hearty, 'Amen.'

Because Jesus cares, he unexpectedly comes alongside us in the storms.

It wasn't so stormy on another occasion, in fact it was a beautiful clear sunny October day some three years BE (Before Evacuation), on the western shore of a quiet Italian seaside village. All our European missionaries working with the Baptist Missionary Society were there for a bit of a rest, teaching, and time to think about what God might be saying to us. I was slowly walking along the beach mulling over some of the things that had been said in the earlier session, and was praying.

Before we went on this retreat we had been having a few questions about a decision we had made a few months earlier. We had felt it right to leave the popular life of the capital and move into a village that many people despised because it was full of gypsies, social rejects and political misfits who had been dumped there by the Communist dictator, Enver Hoxha, in one of his many purges many years before.

Had we done the right thing? I wasn't questioning whether we should have given up a somewhat easier life. It was simply that I felt we were at a crossroads about what we were doing because of how it related to work that had been done previously by some other missionaries.

As I talked to the Lord and tried to listen, my feet and eyes were drawn to the line of seaweed and rubbish that had been brought in and left by the last high tide. While walking along that water-line of odds and ends I picked up a doll's arm, a piece of string all tangled up in the seaweed, and a salty sand-scuffed wooden bead. As I was doing this the Lord unexpectedly came alongside and said, 'I walk the water-line where the flotsam is dumped, and I want you to walk there with me.' And in that short sentence the Lord was clarifying to me that we were in the right place. That's why we love our village, because the Lord loves it and walks there with us.

Someone (actually an Albanian city dweller) later joked with me, saying, 'Here's the gabel (gypsy) of Bregu-i-Lumit.' Far from that being an insult to me I took it not only as a commendation but a confirmation of what had been said to me in that unexpected encounter with the Lord in Italy.

I walk the water-line where the flotsam is dumped.

And now here was Jesus at the lakeside of Galilee, cooking and making fish butties for these failures who had not only let him down at the first sight of blood, and were now running away to the safety of their old lives, but distressed men who had spent a damp and fruitless night trying to succeed at their old way of life. To their shame they couldn't even catch a tiddler to bring home to prove their prowess. And now to cap it all they had failed to recognise who it was on the beach calling to them.

I read an article about a famous film star who turned up unexpectedly at a large hotel in America and was furious that not only did the management fail to recognise him but when he prompted them to think about 'film stars' the owner thought he was someone else. 'I'll never come here again,' he roared as he stormed out of the foyer. Human fame feeds pride, and offended pride can't forgive. But divine fame is humble and forgives, forgives and forgives again. It always says, 'Let's try once more.'

Back on the beach, far from Peter's boat, the famous and familiar Jesus was unknown and unrecognised to those dozy disheartened disciples. Jesus had to do something amazing to jog their memories into life again. So he gave them an unexpected shoal of fish.

Sometimes it's not what the Lord says but what the Lord does that makes us realise that he is with us. We hear his voice but with all the other distracting sounds around us we don't realise it is him until he blows our brains by doing something that says, 'Look folks – it's ME.'

One Sunday I had been preaching at a baptism service in my seaside church in England about 'baptism with water and with the fire' and the power of Jesus. As the service ended and I was talking to the various people who had responded to the call to give their lives to Jesus, one middle-aged member jauntily approached me about a passing comment I had made while inviting people to respond to Jesus. I had said something about those with ailments, and how we would pray for them. He covered himself by saying how he didn't believe 'all this 'ere charismatic stuff and nonsense'. Then a bit flippantly he said, 'I don't suppose anything can be done about my

shoulder?' Catching his mood, and without thinking or
explaining anything, I put my hand near his shoulder
and rather casually said, 'Okay. In the name of Jesus.' To
his surprise, and mine, he jumped a bit and exclaimed
'Ow, that burnt.'

'Then, lift your arm up above your head,' I told him (a
thing he hadn't been able to do for a month or two). Up
it went, without pain or problem, straight as a ramrod.
'That was the fire that I was just preaching about,' I
somewhat sheepishly explained as he turned to push his
way through the crowds around the baptistry who still
wanted to chat with me or with those who had just been
baptised.

'Maybe there is somethin' in all of this,' he stated as he
went back a bit dazed to tell his wife.

The Lord came unexpectedly and did something
surprising to open his eyes, and mine, that said, 'Yes, I
am alive and I am here.'

On another occasion Heather and I were praying for a
lady who had been messed up by things done to her in
her childhood. She had reacted against that experience,
and all sorts of other rejections, with her own form of
rebellion that had at one time even threatened to break
up her marriage. As we prayed with her Jesus came to
her, opened up the door of her hurts and let his pure and
loving healing light shine into her secret darknesses.
What made the difference wasn't our prayer but the fact
that Jesus came and touched her heart. As the tears
rolled down her face she wept and wept in his presence
while he broke and remade her heart.

When Jesus comes, he not only *says* things but he *does*
things – often unexpected things.

He certainly did something for the disciples that they
didn't expect or deserve. And yet even then, after he had
surprised these failed fishermen with a net full of fish, it

was only the one who had spent time with him and got close to him that blurted out, 'It's the Lord.' Probably after a moment or two's thought the other men realised that he was right, so they all bluffly mumbled to one another, 'Mmm. . . why, yes. Of course it is. We thought so all along, didn't we comrades?' And when they all had heartily agreed together that it was Jesus, they pulled on the oars to make for the shore.

But I bet that they wondered what their reception would be like.

Chapter 9

Empty Nets

It was one of those days in Albania. Just typical. Nothing had gone right. The dog had woken up early (and us in the process) and had started barking against the cats that were howling outside – he made his point by weeing in the hall. In sympathy it started raining again, and rainwater once more ran down the walls of our bedroom, hall and kitchen due to the builders having chiselled into and chipped out some of the flat concrete roof above us so as to build a large upstairs room for our church to meet in. Then the carpenters refused to believe that the roof trusses designed by our British architect would hold the roof up. To cap it all one of the neighbours threatened to take us to court for not obtaining his permission to build (despite his other brothers having signed an agreement that it was okay). Besides this there were problems within the church about church members who felt that they should be given a job (preferably paid), and were not happy to be overlooked. With all the damp in our house I had developed a rotten cold and what with the accumulating stress, my blood pressure had rocketed. . . And so it went on.

At such times we ask, 'Why?' Why do such things happen? Why do we experience so many problems? Why do problems seem to multiply like fertile rabbits?

Our Muslim neighbours would say that it is Kismet (Luck) or the will of Allah. Our Calvinist friends (nothing to do with Calvin Klien but a French Christian living in Geneva in the sixteenth century called John Calvin who believed in the absolute sovereignty of God) want to say that that is how things are predestined to be. But are we no more than insignificant objects in the Great Scheme of Things? Are we merely pawns in some great Master Plan? Was it all 'in the plan' that Judas should betray Jesus for a bag of silver? Was it foreordained that Peter would deny any contact with Jesus three times; and were all the close followers of Jesus destined not to be seen for dust when the troops turned up?

It's nice if that is the case, because beliefs like that free us from any accountability and responsibility for our actions. It's almost as good as the humanist position that says we are merely animals – superior maybe – but nonetheless motivated and mobilised by instinct. Therefore we are free from obligation and accountability. The humanist lays the blame for everything at the door of his lower basic instincts; the fatalist as the door of Chance; the Eastern mystic at the conflict of the Ying and Yang; the astrologer at the path of the planets; and those who out-Calvin Calvin, on the total, unalterable and predestined divine plan (which cannot be questioned or changed).

But is that *really* how things work? Are we merely 'puppets on a string' that dance to forces or fates beyond ourselves or who jump to the finger movements of the Great Puppeteer in the sky? Can we so easily excuse failure as part and parcel of the way of life?

It may be a part of life, but I really don't think that God *plans* for us to fail. I believe that we are responsible for how we relate, or refuse to relate to God. I believe that a Christian is someone who is living in a dynamic relationship that shifts and alters according to many circumstances, some of which we choose (a bit like choosing different routes to a final destination that God wants us to eventually arrive at, even if at times it results in us getting stuck up some cul-de-sac). Some things happen because of what we decide. Other times we are forced into circumstances by the choices of *others*.

So why does God allow failure? And why, when we have failed, does he allow failures to multiply? God, it seems, not only *allows* but even *uses* all these things. There is a well-worn phrase in the Bible that says words to the effect that 'every single thing that we come up against clicks together like a jigsaw for the good of those that love, and are loved by, the Lord God'. And that is true despite our inability to see it at times. Can that truth really be applied to our failures? Can failure work for our good? What's so good about failure?

Peter, a long while after this fishing trip, wrote a   letter to Christians worldwide who were going through a lot of pain because of the screw-tightening opposition of the Roman Empire. From his own bitter experience he wryly commented, 'At the time when we are going through all our difficulties, none of it seems very pleasant and it looks like nothing good can come as a result. Well, let me tell you, later it does and. . .'

Really?

What good was there for the three chosen disciples who felt so guilty because they failed Jesus by not standing by him in his hour of need in the garden of Olive Trees? How could it be good for Peter to fail to speak up for Jesus in the High Priest's courtyard? What positive

effect could be found when all of the eleven failed \
believe that Jesus would actually return from the dead?
How was Thomas benefited when he showed himself to
be so stubborn in his disbelief? And now when the seven
went up north for their fishing expedition and feeling so
down, why did they have to experience more failure – a
night of catching nothing but a deeper depression?

I'm a bit of a fisherman, or was in the UK, and so I
understand a little of what fishing is like and how fishermen feel. I remember my sense of personal triumph after
catching my first two small pout whiting on the evening
before our church Harvest of the Sea in the seaport town
of Brixham in Devon. 'Harvest of the Sea' was an annual
event when the church was decorated with fishing
tackle and burgees and packed with 'real' deep sea fishermen who came to thank God for the past year and ask
his help for the next. It was to such a bursting church that
the secretary of the Fishermen's Choir announced my
achievement for everyone to applaud – with a grin.

But more often than not I have trailed my rod and
empty fishing bag back to the car with a sense of disappointment having fished well into the night and lost half
my tackle to the rocks in the depths of the sea off
Brixham's breakwater. When you at last come home,
cold and dispirited, there is no worse answer for a fisherman to have to give in reply to his wife's welcoming
smile and innocent question, 'What did you catch?';
there is nothing so bad as that one, simple, depressing
word, formed through gritted teeth: 'Nothing.' Most
times fishermen are a bit like gamblers: there's always
that sneaking hope which bobs up in the heart like a
fishing float and says, 'Tomorrow. . . maybe it will be the
big one.' But even the most hardy fisherman can get disheartened. Failure compounded by failure can be so
discouraging.

So, why, if God is in charge, does he allow one failure to crash in on top of another like a collapsing house of cards?

One reason is *to catch our attention*. We can be so busy, so self-absorbed and so self-sufficient. How many times as a child did I pull my stubborn little shoulder away from a helping hand and say forcefully, 'Leave me alone. I can do it.'

A little independence is a good thing but not when it blindly refuses all help.

These fishermen thought that they knew a thing or two about the lake that they had worked on all their lives, and they weren't going to listen to a land-lubber carpenter like Jesus when he came into their boat for the first time after a day's preaching.

'We can handle things, Jesus,' they told him firmly. 'You are the teacher; we are the sailors. You've done your bit, now we'll do ours. You just find a nice comfortable cushion and settle down for some shut-eye while we take this boat over to the other side of the water.' That was how they handled Jesus many years before this resurrection event. Basically they were saying to him that as far as boats were concerned they didn't need his help.

It wasn't until the sails were torn, the boat was swamped, and all of them were in danger of drowning, that they woke him up and rather unkindly said, 'Hey, Jesus. Don't you care?'

Did he raise an eyebrow as though to say to them, 'I thought you didn't want me, as a land-lubber, carpenter and teacher to be involved'?

With a slight yawn he slowly got up, looked the storm straight in the eye and said firmly, like one does to an over-enthusiastic yapping puppy, 'Shut up.' And it did. It instantly calmed down.

Gob-smacked they looked at one another, at him, and then back to themselves as they whispered, 'Who on earth is this fellow we've got involved with, that even the winds and waves listen to him and do what he says?'

Amazing isn't it how when people can't cope they either blame God, even if they haven't given a thought to him since the last funeral service they went to, or, on the other hand, more surprisingly, start to pray. How many times do we read, in those 'human tragedy' articles that the Readers' Digest is fond of printing, of people suddenly discovering or remembering the importance of prayer.

Does God allow problems to waft over lives so as to catch our attention?

It's a thought.

* * *

Then failure teaches us *about our weaknesses*.

Peter learned a life-changing lesson on another occasion, when Jesus had walked across the waves to them during a storm. In amazement, and probably without thinking, as usual, Peter asked Jesus to allow him to step out onto the water and to have the same sort of miraculous feet as Jesus. Flushed with success as he walked to Jesus, he thought he had cracked it. Walking on water was a doddle. 'Look at me folks, I'm a water walker', his bragging swaggering attitude boasted. . . that is until the water started to rise up round his ankles, shins, knees and hips!

'Hang on, something's going wrong!' a little voice inside him must have yelled to his stupid brain.

But it was not 'something', it was 'someone'. It was Peter himself that was to blame. Peter realised too late that he was only able to keep on top of things by the power of Jesus, not his own will power.

Too many people these days are being conned into trusting in the unlimited inner resources that can be released by believing in oneself. 'Self-realisation' and 'the power of positive thought' is what they are told to have faith in. 'Mind over matter' and 'mind control' can all too easily slip into an 'external power' control that can be demonic. By all means we need to know ourselves and stretch ourselves, but also we need to realise that we are weak and faulty! People can rise to such amazing heights but then can crash to such appalling depths. As Paul said, 'It's only by the undeserved kindness and love of God that I am what I am.'

But it was Peter himself that was to blame.

Peter was walking on the water not because of his ability to tap in to the energy levels of his own inner self but by responding to the invitation and power of Jesus. So Jesus allowed Peter to fail (in front of a sniggering bunch of workmates) to teach him an unforgettable lesson. Many years later, when writing his first letter to all the young Christian believers he felt a concern for in Turkey, he recalled this event and wrote about the principle that he had learned that day. He wrote, 'We are kept up on top of things, and we are kept going, only by the power of God.'

Most of us don't like to find out, and even less to *talk* about, our weaknesses. And yet, that can be the most helpful thing not only for us to keep in mind for our own welfare but also for the instruction and encouragement of others.

I will never forget the impact that one book had on me in the 1970s. It was the era when everyone seemed to be writing about their power encounters with God and how their lives had been totally changed for the better. It seemed, at that time, as though everything in life could be transformed by a newly discovered ability to praise the Lord for every circumstance and situation. Mice could become men, and men could become giants who would conquer the world, naturally and spiritually, for the Lord. In those days of the seventies you were made to feel a total failure if you dared to omit the obligatory 'Praise the Lord' or 'Hallelujah' almost every other word. You certainly didn't dare ever mention that you weren't happy or you were worried about something. And then like a brilliant shaft of light there exploded across my life a book written by David Watson – a man in the forefront of renewal and someone experiencing a powerful healing ministry not only in his home church in York but throughout the world.

In his book *You are my God* he wrote with transparent honesty about his personal struggles with sickness and failure, and how at times he had to battle with that unmentionable thing called 'depression'. At last, I felt, here was a man I could get near to.

This was a man on my own wavelength. Those other Christians, constantly looking like grinning gargoyles, frightened me off. What would they say if they saw that I was wearing a crumbling mask of hard-attempted unending joy in the Lord? I was worried that they might find out that my gaily painted mask was tied on with a slowly fraying thread. This man, by taking off his mask, drew me close to him with such honesty. But more important than that he drew me to the one he loved and served. Through the writings of David Watson, Jesus came to me as a doctor for the sick, not as a personal trainer of those in perfect health. He was seen as the saviour who came not for the strong but the weak, as the helper not of the successful but the failures.

Failure teaches us about our inadequacies. Moses passed on God's reason for allowing the Israelites to go through the scrag lands of the Negev for forty years instead of by the direct route. He explained why God let them get uncomfortable and hungry. 'I did it to show you what was going on in your hearts,' God said. The Lord was trying them out so as to show them (not him) how weak and incapable they were to make it on their own.

Difficulties expose our weaknesses.

And that's not a bad thing.

* * *

Another reason God allows failure is *to strip away our pride*.

When Peter so forcefully swore (literally, with a few of his old-fashioned, well-used, fisherman's curses that he had suppressed for the past three years) that he had nothing to do with Jesus and Dr Luke says, 'the Lord looked on Peter', that look wasn't to say, 'I told you so.' It was to make Peter aware of the things that he had warned him about, the pitfall of pride that he would fall into, and about the weakness in his own nature. That look of Jesus was the sad expression that said, 'Oh, Peter.' That's what broke Peter's heart.

Teenagers feel that they need to make a good impression. I was no exception when I entered those explosive, confusing and sensitive years. I wanted to impress people with my coolness and capability. But on one unforgettable occasion it didn't quite work out as I intended. After a nasty storm I was helping my father to sort out our boat that was moored on the mud flats of the Thames Estuary at Southend. Many boats had sunk at their moorings. Ours had done better than most. She had shipped plenty of water but had ridden out the storm despite being half submerged.

Her engine was of course completely flooded, and so together Dad and I were spending the long hours when the tide was out taking the engine carefully apart, cleaning and drying it, and putting it together again. The sparking plug which had been removed earlier was resting on the side of the boat, but with all the vibration of Dad moving around inside the boat the plug had rolled off and fallen in the mud – and Southend has plenty when the tide goes out (it's not called Sa'fend-on-Mud by the locals for nothing!).

'I'll get it,' I said, eager to show my usefulness. But as I attempted to turn towards it my feet wouldn't move. My wellies were firmly stuck in the black goo. So, like in a slow-motion film, having lost my centre of gravity, my body slowly continued to bend in the direction I had tried to turn until, like a felled tree, I crashed, face down, into the black sticky mud.

I arose looking like one of the black and white minstrels that were popular on TV at the time. There was no water to wash in, so with the hot sun my face and my pullover became firmly hardened with sun-baked mud. But worse was to come. Not only did we have to walk back to the car along a crowded promenade but then my Dad drove back home at what seemed to be about

10 mph with me like some royal figure having to stand up at the back of his open-top car so as not to spoil the seat! So much for coolness – more like comedy – as people stopped, pointed, stared and sniggered at this apparition in black and white.

I crashed, face down, into the black mud.

We have a lovely verse about God's faithfulness and help in our Albanian Bible that translates literally as, 'I will not leave you in the mud.' I note that it doesn't say, 'I won't let you fall in the mud or get splattered and covered with it', just, 'I won't ever leave you in it'!

God, it seems, allows us to get muddy so as to get rid of our pride.

At our last church in the UK (the one that sent us abroad), during a time of prayer when a group of us were trying to hear from God, one of the young wives was given a phrase by the Lord for us to think about – 'All pride gone.' Again and again the Bible tells us that there is no place for pride in the hearts of those who would follow Jesus. Certainly not the sort of pride that Peter showed when he criticised the unreliability of the other disciples of Jesus while boasting about his own dependability.

'Oh yes, Lord, *they* will fail you when the time of testing comes, but not me. I'm ready to die for you,' he bragged.

'Don't be so cock-sure Peter,' Jesus warned, '. . . and talking of which, before the cock crows to welcome in tomorrow's sunrise, three times you'll have said that you don't have anything to do with me.'

And that's exactly what happened. As a result of his big mouth bragging about his faithfulness and then betraying his friend, this burly fisherman, broken of pride, broke down in the dark and cried his eyes out.

So much for pride.

Was that why Peter later wrote in one of his letters, 'God is dead set against pride. He wants to pull it down.'

* * *

Another good purpose that rides in on the back of failure is that God can use it *to teach us new things*.

When as a young child I did something wrong, like hitting my thumb with a hammer, my Dad used to say, 'Son, you don't want to do that.'

Gradually I learned by my mistakes that there was another and better way.

The disciples who opted out of the 'Mountain-Top Prayer Meeting' wished they had been there for at least two reasons. First, after hearing from Peter, James and John about the miraculous change that came over Jesus; the appearance of the Old Testament Shining Cloud around them that in earlier times showed the Israelites that the presence of Almighty God was with them, and their seeing Moses and Elijah; and then how they actually heard the voice of God, oh, they wished they'd been there. But secondly, and more pragmatically, they'd

wished they'd gone with Jesus because left alone they
had got stuck with a problem that they couldn't cope
with, and very soon thought that they'd have been
better to have not got involved with in the first place.

While Jesus was there on the mountain-top, a dad had
turned up with his young son obviously under the control of something evil. The boy kept throwing himself
into the fire, or into water in an attempt to end his young
life. The boy's dad asked for help, but despite all their
earlier experiences – successes that had made them feel
they would be able to cope with just about anything –
they soon discovered that they couldn't deal with this
problem on their own.

A bit shamed-faced when Jesus came down from the
mountain, they had to ask him for his help, and he got
rid of the evil spirit immediately.

'Why couldn't we do that?' they asked. 'We've done it
before in your name.'

Jesus simply replied, 'Because of your lack of prayer
and your little faith.'

Ouch! That must have hit them hard after their refusal
to go with Jesus up the mountain for a prayer time.
Then, when they had calmed down a bit, Jesus went on
to talk to them about spiritual battles and the need to
fast and pray.

The turning point in their lives was this – Failure.
Failure led to questions, questions to honest answers,
and honest answers to important lessons that needed to
be learned.

Sometimes through failure we learn something about
ourselves, sometimes something new about God, and
sometimes things about both. It must have been three or
four years before we were sent out to Albania that I was
at a clergy conference arranged by St Andrew's Church
in Chorleywood under the leadership of Bishop David

Pytches. An American church leader called Brent Rue was talking to some five hundred British church leaders about prophecy. At the end of the day he said something about how he felt that a demonstration of the way in which this gift worked might be helpful. He then singled out five people to whom he gave words that he felt were from God.

I was one of the five.

A number of things were said to me that deeply impacted my life. He said that in his mind God gave him an impression about me. 'I saw you like somebody at a tennis match, and you're one that was . . . oh you're such a fan, and you love to go to all the tennis matches, and you love to play tennis, and you're just having such a great time at it, but you had no idea they were going to put you on the professional circuit. And you say, oh I can't, er-r, I'm a fan, not a real player – I do it recreationally. Now the Lord says, "That is how I see you in the kingdom", because your heart is very transparent to Jesus. Because of the way that you view the kingdom, life and ministry, the Lord says, "I'm moving you into places that you would be frightened in your own ability to do. It's way over my head, well, I couldn't do this."

'Let me just say this,' he continued. 'If the Lord brings opportunities, know that he doesn't want to change you. It is because he has fashioned and formed you for the ministry to conform around you. The strength you have is who you are in Christ, and he can take you in many doors because of that one.'

First of all there was something in that word that spoke to my immediate situation. I was, at the time, questioning the manner and method of my ministry. And here was God immediately answering this problem by saying, 'I don't want you to change.'

Then he talked about 'moving you into places that you would be frightened in your own ability to do'. That just about summed up my feeling regarding our leaving the UK for Albania some three years later. As I approached my fiftieth birthday, and had to attempt to learn what some linguists say is one of the top five hardest languages to master, it was certainly going to be 'way over my head' – and I'm still struggling with the Albanian language many years further down the road!

But it is the evacuation experience that's the mindblower. Brent began his word to me seven years before by saying this, 'The Lord is just showing me that there are surprises in store for you. That the surprises have to do with the way you view God and the way that you're going to see that he views you. And there are things that he has put in your nature and your personality that are precious to him.' In the failure of leaving Albania I was to gain a new understanding of myself as God sees me. I was to learn that I am weak and failing – despite so many years of teaching about discipleship, obedience and following the Lord. Over the years I had come to think how strong I was. But through that evacuation experience I have now come to see that in times of difficulty I am as capable as the next person of running away rather than running to the Lord. That surprised me and humbled me.

But then with that failure has also come the overwhelming sense that my Lord Jesus is kind, patient, forgiving and generous. He not only surrounded me when I was running away, but gave me a second chance to return and start again. But more of that later.

It must have been a bit like that for Peter. When Jesus warned him about the danger that was looming on the horizon he said, 'Peter, despite the difficulties you're going to have to face and disaster that will come crashing down on you, I have prayed for you that, even though you may fail, your faith won't.

'Oh, and by the way Peter,' Jesus went on, 'when it's all over and you have come to a new understanding of yourself and me, you will then be able to give real strength to others.'

He didn't say, 'If you overcome you'll be a great saint and a wonderful example of faith.' Nor did he say, 'If you fail me you'll have blown it and be of no further use to me.' What he said was 'When you turn away and then turn back, by confession and change, you'll be even more useful.'

Peter through his failure came to learn not only about his own weakness but, at the same time, a lot more about the amazing love of the Lord.

Chapter 10

Safety at Last

We have a dog in our home in Albania. He is an Albanian dog called Roy (which in Albanian means 'a guard'). And he is crazy – probably from living with us and having to be bilingual. Every so often he has a wild turn. His eyes go glazed, his ears cocked at half mast, neither up nor down, and suddenly he charges round in circles trying to catch his own tail. When he does eventually get hold of his tail he looks at us sheepishly, with

Failure makes you go round in circles – a bit like chasing your own tail.

delight, as he hangs on to it for dear life. But more often than not he ends up with a soppy, cross-eyed look on his face as he stands there dizzily panting with nothing in his mouth but a drooling tongue.

Many people are like that with failure. It leaves them dizzy and exhausted. Failure makes you go round in circles – a bit like chasing your own tail, or is it your tail chasing you? My father had a wicked sense of humour. Every Christmas all the family, ours and his sister's and brother's, would meet at his parents (my grandparents) for the annual viewing of the movie films that my Dad had taken throughout the years. Great would be the hoots of laughter at the mild rebuke of his mother when he would suddenly stop the film and put it in reverse. Instead of my cousin stuffing trifle *into* his mouth he would be seen gleefully taking it out. Instead of me wobbling on a bicycle going *forwards* I would be seen struggling to pedal backwards. Instead of my childhood dog (not our Albanian one) chasing his tail his tail would be chasing him.

That's a bit like what can happen with failure. At times everything seems to go in reverse and instead of us being in control we find that things are controlling us. It's as though instead of us wagging our tail, *it* takes over and chases us, gets a hold of us, shakes us around, and we can't get away from it.

Failure very often can turn into a cyclical thing. I fail. I think I am a failure and will fail again. I then fail, and say to myself, 'I thought I would,' adding 'and I will probably do it again.' Then I do, and so it goes on and on, round and round. . . Eventually we see everything through the two lenses of gloom and doom that are fitted into the dark glasses of failure.

Is that how Peter and the Galilee Fishermen's Club felt? Is that the impact behind the words, 'And that night

they caught nothing.' Did they look blearily at one
another as the morning sky began to fleck with grey,
with hunched shoulders, and say, 'Oh no, not more
problems and disappointments. Will nothing ever go
right for us?'

In failure we often feel like that – we've got the
reverse Midas touch. Everything we touch turns to gran-
ite not gold.

How can that change, if it can? How do we break
through the fog that failure stirs up in order to arrive at
a clear and lasting security?

From looking at all the questions asked on that day in
Galilee we can learn a number of lessons.

Jesus stood on the beach and first of all got them *to
admit their problem*.

'Have you caught anything?' was more than an interest question, after all Jesus knew anyway (like he knew
what Thomas had said about not believing until he put
his finger in the holes that the Roman nails had made in
Jesus' hands). Jesus so often starts the process of healing
by getting us to say how it is, to admit our failures without fear, and then to tell him that we've made a bit of a
mess of things.

In May 1997, a short while after our evacuation from
the anarchy in Albania, my wife and I found ourselves
crying our way through most of our national denomin-
ational annual assembly. Ironically, for us, it had been
given the title 'Taking the Risk' – the very thing that we
felt we had failed to do by leaving Albania. We felt devastated as the congregation lustily and, at the time we
felt, superficially sang those well-known words of Isaac
Watts that end, 'Love so amazing, so divine, demands
my soul, my life, my all.' With what integrity could we
now sing those words when we had opted out of such
demands? How could we honestly share in the theme

song written by Christopher Idle for the Assembly, *And did you risk yourself, O Christ?*

It was a hymn to remind people about saints of old who risked their lives for Christ. It spoke about the sparse news of people today who risk all for Jesus, whether by prison, torture, or death. It called people to release things that undermined the task of kingdom-growth and anything that contradicts our creed.

As the organ swelled in the last verse people sang about renouncing rights of choice to hear and follow the Lord. The organ reached a crescendo as people concluded with gusto

'Can this be risk, to die to rise with you, our Glory Song?'

Think about those words from our point of view. Choked with emotion the words literally stuck in our throats. Unable to sing such contradictions, we just cried and cried with confusion, guilt and pain.

Two special friends from our earlier Devon days saw our distress after one of the sessions and took us to an old-fashioned pub round the corner from the great and imposing Westminster Central Hall. As we drank coffee, hot chocolate and some cider (not all together) they got us to pour out what was going on inside. Out tumbled all our evacuation experience and our feelings of failure. Patiently they listened, then after a long while they, in a simple and uncomplicated way, brought us back to the heart of the Christian message – that the cross brings forgiveness for failures.

'If you feel that you did wrong, simply tell it to the Lord and receive his forgiveness,' was Derek's wise advice, reminding us once again of the fantastic news that Christians have but so often find hard to apply.

On more than one occasion Jesus talked about how he came not for people who had it all together but for those who hadn't – a bit like a doctor who helps sick people not fit ones.

The doctor image is a useful analogy. The doctor probes and asks, 'What's going on? What has happened? What are the symptoms?' and things like, 'Where does it hurt? When did it start?'

It's no good when the doctor greets you and asks, 'How are you?' to reply 'Fine thanks', or he will say something like, 'Then why are you wasting my time?' The path of healing is not to pretend everything is okay. We have to stop and ask some important questions and then give some honest answers.

First of all we have to admit that we have a problem.

During the time when Albania was full of guns we nearly had a blood feud in our village between some of our neighbours after a young man, who was in our church, offended a young girl by saying that he would marry her if no one else would have her. Not the most tactful way of putting it! And he didn't help his case later by teasing her.

As a result a friend of hers caught the 'offending' young man in the dark one night, beat him up, and put him in hospital. Albanian custom dictates that revenge must be taken for something like that, and we knew that there were plenty of weapons in both their homes.

What a twenty-four hours I spent talking with all those involved. Thank God I was helped by Fredi, a wise Christian Albanian young man from the capital, who had worked with us earlier in our church for a period of about six months. We spoke to each one of the people caught up in this complicated mess about admitting their faults. We then told them that Christianity is all about forgiving one another. We reminded all the three families involved that only God, who knows all the facts, has the right to take vengeance. By the end of an exhausting day, going backwards and forwards from one house to another, the immediate danger was defused.

The basic problem was that although everyone could easily see the faults of the others, they found it very difficult to admit their own. In the end, the first lad (who had done the teasing) was eventually prepared to admit he did some things wrong and was ready to ask forgiveness. But the girl refused, and still does, either to forgive him, let him talk to her, or to ask for forgiveness for her part in it all. She kept saying to us, 'I'm without fault. I've a clean heart. I'm perfect.' Sadly her friend who jumped to her defence, although saying sorry with his mouth, didn't show it in his attitude or in his heart either.

Theirs was not the way to get out of the hole that they had all dug for themselves. The only way out of the Failure Maze is to stop. To stop getting deeper into the maze and to say, 'I've got a problem here. I've got myself into a mess.'

That's why Jesus asked, 'Have you caught anything?'

And he wanted an honest answer from them – like he does from us.

* * *

The next lesson that I get from John's story about Jesus and the disappointed all-night fishermen is this:

The way to break through the failure cycle is *to learn to trust*.

Failure often robs us of trust. We don't trust ourselves, what we are or what we do, and along with that find it hard to trust others.

When I was young, for a birthday present, I was given a series of horse-riding lessons along with the girl next door. After my friend was introduced to a patient white mare that nuzzled her hand affectionately, I was led to a big huge black stallion (fifteen hands high) that had fire in his eyes, and on whose back I looked no more than an irritating pimple. It wasn't surprising that at one point when we were trotting through the woods in convoy my horse decided, despite all my efforts to the contrary, to break out into a gallop, bouncing me about on his back like an upside down yo-yo. As he went down. . . I went up, as he rose up. . . I came down for another painful encounter. This continued for a while until the inevitable happened. I lost my footing in the stirrup and so, as I was bounced up for the umpteenth time I found myself catapulted through the air and over his neck when he suddenly came to a stop. Like in those cartoon films I seemed to hang there in space for a few a seconds with his reigns in my hand, then gravity took over. Although he had come to an abrupt halt, I hadn't, and continued on until with a crash I hit the ground in front of him. Stars flashed before my eyes as I gasped for breath. The riding instructor rushed over to check me out, gave the horse a whipping (which I later thought was a bit unfair), and then carefully put me back on.

I could have finished my riding days there and then, but through the action of my instructor I learned two things. One. If you get back on something (be it horse or bike or whatever) immediately after you have fallen off, you learn the lesson of renewed trust and how not to lose your confidence. Two. If you fall off a horse and get back on again you can ride back to the stables with your head on the shoulder of a young and pretty instructor!

How many people have had an accident of some sort, when learning to swim, for example. Maybe they were let go of, or slipped through their rubber ring, and frantically gasping for air they've eventually surfaced, never to risk swimming again. Perhaps they haven't fallen off a horse but a bike or skateboard and because they didn't get back on immediately, have never ridden again.

How many people after a failed business venture find it hard to start up again. They don't trust themselves, they don't trust other people, or they don't trust the system any more.

So often, as a 'soft-touch' clergyman, I could have said, when people have disappeared over the horizon with money that they have borrowed from me, 'I'll never listen to anyone's hard-luck story again.' But I haven't – though I am a little more careful since.

How many men or women after a broken friendship, or fractured marriage relationship, say that they feel they can never trust anyone else again. They have lost their nerve. They are suspicious of things, people, and even their own ability to cope.

Jesus was basically asking these fishermen after a night of failure, 'Will you learn to trust me and my advice when everything shouts against it?'

In effect that's what Jesus had said some time earlier to one of the motley crew in the boat – doubting Thomas – who even now was probably sitting glumly in the boat saying, 'I knew we wouldn't catch anything. Life's a bummer.' Only a week or so before this time on the beach Jesus had said to him, 'Those who have not seen me eye to eye and *yet have believed* are the ones who God is pleased with. They are the ones who will be lastingly and really happy.'

As I was preparing this part of the book the news broke that the old crooner himself, Frank Sinatra, had just died. Probably the most famous song that he ever sang is one that says he did it his way. It's good enough to be the theme song of all those who don't follow Jesus.

It rings an all too familiar chord in our proud, independent and sinful hearts.

Albanian young people love the imported music of the West, even though they don't always understand it. The evening chatter of older people by their doorways, and the laughter of children playing with a punctured football along the dusty roads is often shattered by music blaring from a dented wreck of a car reverberating with one of their favourite songs by The Pet Shop Boys, *It's My Life*.

Jesus in contrast to those two phrases says, 'It's not your life, it's mine. Don't do it your way, do it my way. Trust me even if you feel it's not worth it, even if you think that nothing will come of it.'

How often Jesus, during his lifetime in Palestine, looked for, pointed to, and commended people for their faith. There was a Roman officer who, though an outsider to the Jewish religion, one day asked Jesus for help for one of his sick servants. Jesus said about that officer, 'I've never found so much faith here in Israel, not even in those chosen ones who have all the heritage and benefits of God's activity and promises.' To a Jewish leader, whose daughter was terminally ill and in fact died when Jesus was on the way to help her, Jesus said just two challenging words, 'Trust me.'

That's not easy. How can you trust when the little bit of faith that you have has just been blown out the window by things getting worse rather than better?

This leader's desperate heart cry is very special to me because his simple request was the only prayer that I could pray as cancer raged through the body of my young daughter. 'Jesus,' I cried, 'come and touch my little girl who is at the point of death.' Hard as it was to hear from God after her hasty death, all I could hold on to in the darkness that engulfed me in death's Shadow Valley were those two words, 'Trust Me.' Yet how hard it was to continue to trust as I slipped into the quagmire of depression.

Some seven months later a sort of turning point came in my heart at the first Good Friday service following her death. I went with my wife to the local parish church, in the village where we were staying, for a three-hour service for that special day that was to be led by the Bishop of Salisbury. The first hour focused on 'the Word', when the story of the sufferings of Christ were read, dramatised and talked about. The last hour was directed to 'Enactment' and 'Eucharist' (which comes from the Greek and means 'thanksgiving'). That was when we shared in bread and wine while celebrating Christ's Last Supper together. The central hour, however, majored on 'Worship'. The bishop invited us, while we in the congregation sang or just the choir led in song or the organ played appropriate music, to come (whenever we felt it appropriate) and stand, kneel or prostrate ourselves in prayer around a ten foot cross. This rough wooden cross had been carried during the period of Lent to the various churches through the valley and at this point in the service it was brought in and set up at the front of our church.

As soon as we started to sing in that central session, even before people began to go forward, tears began to slowly burn down my cheeks as my raw heart started to break open. Eventually I went forward with heaving shoulders, knelt at that cross, and wept for a long while. Something struggled inside me as I thought of the suffering of Jesus who cried in the darkness, just like me, 'God, where are you in all of this?' I wept for some twenty or so minutes until I eventually sobbed out from my heart as a sort of prayer, 'Your will, not mine be done.'

The tears didn't stop, the pain didn't go, the darkness didn't lift, in fact it was another year before I was declared medically okay, but I believe that at that point a crossroads was passed.

Faith, I have painfully come to experience, somehow holds on when everything else has gone. Faith is a bit like a sightless bat – it just hangs in there, even in the dark.

Trust is a hard lesson that we all have to learn, and it isn't real until it's tested. However when it is used it becomes the main exit door out of the long corridor of disappointment and failure.

'Drop your nets in on the starboard side of your boat and you *will* find something,' Jesus authoritatively said to these weary anglers.

'What again?' Peter probably inwardly groaned.

I wonder what I would have done if I'd been down on the quayside at Brixham and, after a weary night of useless fishing, a stranger had turned up just as I was packing up all my tackle to go home for breakfast and he said, 'One more cast; just there,' and it was the same place where I'd been fruitlessly trying to catch fish all night.

What did the men in the boat turn to and trust in after that long night of wasted energy? It wasn't their instincts, abilities and experience. No, it was this stranger's compelling words.

Sometimes Jesus asks us to do the oddest and most irrational of things. On other occasions he asks us to just keep on keeping on with the same old faith. At other times it's to venture out with a new sort of faith that will overcome all the failures of the past.

But through it all he is simply saying 'Trust me.'

* * *

The third thing Jesus calls for is *obedience*.

The most obvious, simple and basic way out of failure, after admitting what's gone wrong, is to get back on track. It's through renewed obedience that we move out of the shadow of failure.

That can be costly.

We had to count the cost not only of failure in our Albanian situation but of subsequent obedience to the Lord. The problem was that our missionary organisation, which has had many years of experience with similar situations (more recently in Africa and Asia and earlier in China, and all the circumstances in between), felt that we should not return to the dangers and uncertainties in Albania at that particular moment. We appreciated their concern for us. We acknowledged that they also had prayed through the political and spiritual situation as it had developed and we accepted the fact that they had to consider a wider perspective.

In one sense they were trapped in a catch-22 situation – whatever they decided to do or not do they would be criticised for it. If they had left their missionaries out on a limb or, what was worse, actually sent them back to face danger and someone was killed, they'd have been harshly criticised for doing wrong. On the other hand if they pulled everyone out, and kept them out, and the whole situation had quietly blown over, they'd have been accused of being panickers, money wasters, and worse than that, of 'not trusting the Lord' (which is an easy thing to say to a missionary society from the comfort of an armchair in a semi-detached somewhere in the leafy lanes of suburban Great Britain).

Hindsight is always more sharply focused than foresight!

In all this we also understood the advice given to us by those Christians who said that we were 'under authority' and should submit to our Society's prayerful authority. That just made the whole scenario more painful as we loved and respected the people who were over us. Throughout my ministry in various churches I also had preached on the Christian's call to submission. Someone who knew me rather well and remembered some of those words bluntly told me, 'Now the shoe is on the other foot. Do what you are told.'

But as Albania fell apart and we sat in the comfort and peace of our two daughters' homes, *daily* the Lord spoke to us through the Bible, through comments in our Bible notes, through many tugs on our heart-strings, through visions, through friends, even through a stained glass church window, to go back.

A matter of days after our arrival in the UK in our daily Bible readings in Isaiah we came across chapter 48, verse 18 (following the Scripture Union's passages set for us for each day - not selectively picking out those sorts of verses that we wanted to find), this verse hit us like a bolt out of the blue as we struggled with our troubled consciences. 'If you had listened to what I had told you then your peace would have been like refreshing rivers of water.'

A most poignant comment cropped up another day later on. Our Bible notes were reflecting on Abraham's detour from faith in Genesis. The commentator writing on that particular passage said bluntly that if we had 'taken a wrong direction' then we ought 'to go back' to where we had gone wrong 'and start again'.

One afternoon, exhausted with all these inner struggles, we went into our local village parish church in Dorset where we were staying to pray through our predicament. After grappling for a long time in prayer about what God really wanted us to do, my wife pointed up at the beautiful stained glass window just where we *happened* to be kneeling. We were blown away by the words at the bottom that said, 'Be thou faithful unto death and I will give thee a crown of life.'

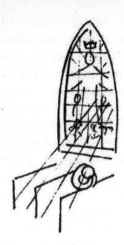

The Lord spoke to us . . . even through a stained glass church window

Like a flash my mind went back over the many years I had served the Lord as a pastor. I thought about the great number of people that I had baptised as believers – people saying that they were ready to follow Jesus as Lord – and had baptised them with those very words from the book of Revelation. I recalled the many times that I had preached on the damning statement of Samuel to Saul when as King he did something outside the will of God: 'To obey God fully and completely is much better than sacrificing things to him, and to listen to the Lord is more important than the best and costliest worship that we can give him.' How often I had spoken on the words of Peter a couple of months after this lakeside encounter with his risen, and now ascended, Lord. Standing before the Jewish Council, which questioned his authority for healing a lame man in the Temple precincts, he made the simple statement, 'We ought to obey God rather than men.' I had constantly taught throughout my ministry in the UK and Albania that discipleship means, 'Following and obeying Jesus . . . whatever.' My wife and I had sung from the earliest days in our first church, 'If no one joins me still I will follow. No turning back. No turning back.' In the church that we had started before going to Albania one of the values we accepted there was 'to allow people to do what they believe the Lord is saying', even if they were wrong, because the Lord can teach open minds but can't do anything with closed hearts. And then I reflected in my mind how in Albania as new Christians stood on the sandy beach waiting to be baptised I would ask each one the same question, 'Are you ready to follow Jesus, whatever it may cost you?' So what should we do now?

I felt I had failed the Lord once by leaving Albania. Now that I had asked for his forgiveness did I dare disobey him a second time? There was more than my job on the line (after all, we reasoned, we could be dismissed by our Society for going against it and doing our own thing – which graciously the people in our mission HQ afterwards did not do - but it was a possibility). The fact was, I believed that my whole Christian life and ministry was on the line at this point. If I didn't obey now I felt that not only would I have to give up being a missionary but that I could never open my mouth again to talk about Christian things. . . ever!

It was 'crisis of conscience' day for us. Would we do what we believed God was saying to us or not?

Jesus said two things to Peter on *his* special day down on the beach in Galilee that both basically meant, 'Try again.' The first thing, I believe, was a preparation for the second. To start with Jesus, the unknown stranger, said, 'Drop your nets on the starboard side, and you'll catch something.' What crazy advice! After all, they had been doing that very thing throughout the whole of the night and caught nothing. Nevertheless, Jesus expects us to obey, whatever we may have done in the past, and especially when we have lost our nerve through failure. He says, 'Try, try again.' However, this time it was more than a matter of trial and error, it was a matter of obedience. That's what brought them eventual success.

The nets that they wearily but obediently threw out and the fish that they caught were evidence of the lordship of Jesus. That's why the question that was in everyone's mind, 'Who is it?' was never voiced. John says why no one said it. 'They all knew it was the Lord.'

The second thing was more personal for Peter. Jesus took Peter on one side and said to him at the end of a painful 'question and answer' session, 'Peter, follow me.' Bells must have rung in Peter's troubled mind when he heard those words. It didn't take him long to remember that that was exactly how he had started with Jesus some three years earlier. It was with a similar call. Maybe he was standing at that selfsame spot on the beach where Jesus had first said to him, 'Follow me.' Now Jesus was saying it all over again, 'Peter, will you follow me?'

We humans have a tendency to complicate the things of God and cloud the issues till we can't see the wood for the trees. Some people in the church make Christianity so hard, when in fact it is basically simple. The start, heart and finishing point of the Christian message is summed up in those two words: 'Follow me.'

Peter eventually got the message. Later on he wrote in his first letter about the need to 'follow in the steps of Jesus' even when it's painful and costly because that's what Christians are 'called to do'.

That was the thing that became the nub of the issue for us and our return to Albania. So, after much asking, writing and telephoning our HQ without getting them to change their minds, I caught the train up to London, bought two plane tickets back to Albania, and the next day we were there back in our village, surrounded by our church family and friends.

Once again we called the church together, only this time to ask them to forgive us for being a bad example to the young believers in our village. We told them to keep their eyes on Jesus not us.

What I actually said that June Sunday in 1997 was:

First: Sorry.

We are sorry that we are not a good example. We haven't a good conscience about when we left Albania. We did two wrong things:

a. We didn't pray when the British Embassy said 'Leave.'

b. We didn't ask you, as our spiritual family, for your thoughts

So we say, 'Sorry.' This was a problem because we told you that we would not go, we thought that it was right to stay, but we listened to our authorities more than Jesus.

Second: We are here again.

We are here again because Jesus told us to leave England. We have come because we must obey the Lord more than people.

We are sorry that we are late, but we are here.

What joy, what peace, and what a sense of assurance filled our hearts because at last we could once again look up into the face of our patient and forgiving Master and worship him with a clear conscience. We felt that even if we were to be shot the next day by one of the guns that were constantly echoing round our village (and a bullet, that I've still got, did land a few feet away from us one day while we were in the garden) whatever might happen we knew that we could face the Lord with a clear conscience at last. We felt that we could happily say to him that we had done what we believed he had told us to do. It was a relief to have got it all cleared up.

One Sunday, a month or so after our return, towards the end of a service in which I was talking about the 'Runaway Eleven' who forsook Jesus before he was arrested in the Garden of Olive Trees, a young man who was in our little church for the first time stood up and said, 'Excuse me, can I ask a question?'

'Yes,' I replied. 'Go ahead.'

'You are talking about following Jesus and how his friends ran away and left him. Why did you run away and leave us when things got tough?'

Despite the defensiveness of those members who wanted him to sit down and shut up, I was able to answer his question with honesty and a peaceful heart.

'Yes, we had been like the disciples and run away,' I confessed. 'It's easy to do things like that under pressure. But,' I pointed out, to the accompanying nods of everyone there, 'we returned to Albania to ask for forgiveness from the Lord Jesus and his family here.

'This is the heart of the good news of the Christian faith,' I continued. 'We all fail. But when we say sorry God is willing to forgive. That's why Jesus came and died on the cross - to pay for our wrongs and give us a new start.

'I'm ready to follow Jesus again. What about you?' I threw out, as a challenge.

Although he left at that point, others in the church followed up the wonderful news that we have to offer, and praise God there were those that day who said that they wanted to trust and follow Jesus for themselves.

God loves failures, forgives failures, and gives failures a new start. Wow!!

* * *

To overcome failure we also need *to learn the lesson of love*.

When all the catch was safely landed Jesus called over the tired fishermen to join him and have some breakfast he had prepared. God is so practical when he sees our weaknesses. Moral and spiritual weaknesses can at times be connected to the root of something physical. To depressed Elijah the Lord sent an angel with some food and then put him to sleep for a bit. For the five thousand men (plus women and children) after a long day of listening to his teaching Jesus provided a massive meal from five small rolls and two tiddly sardines. That miracle produced so many leftovers that the disciples filled twelve fishing baskets with the leftovers when Jesus told them to tidy up. Twelve baskets – one for each of them that doubted! To the excited parents of the twelve-year-old girl that Jesus had brought back to life he said, 'Don't just stand there grinning, give the child a sandwich.' So now, after a wasted night of expended energy and then the exhilaration of a miraculous catch, Jesus' first thought was to give these over-tired and over-excited fishermen something to eat.

It was after the meal was over, when everyone was stretching themselves on the beach and picking the bones out from between their teeth that Peter saw a beckoning finger and thought, 'Oh, oh. This is it!'

As he and Jesus wandered alone along the beach together, Jesus stopped, put his hand on Peter's shoulder, looked him straight in the eye, and asked, 'Peter, do you love me more than all the others over there?'

With a quick look around to make sure that this time no one was listening he said a weak, 'Uh huh.'

'Peter,' Jesus asked a bit further on, 'Now let's get this cleared up. Do you remember saying that you loved me enough to die for me? Is that really how you feel about me?'

'Oh, why did Jesus have to have such perfect recall?' Peter must have thought to himself.

'Well. . . it's like this. . . you are my special friend.'

'Peter,' Jesus asked a third time, 'am I really that special to you?'

'Lord you know everything. . . You know all that's in my heart,' Peter said with a lump in his throat.

What was Jesus getting at by all those questions – besides making Peter face up to his earlier claims that he had in the moment of testing forgotten? It was basically the fact that Jesus is more interested in our *relationship* with him, than all the good and right things that we might *do* for him.

Once Jesus had blasted away the self-confidence of the people who were crowding round him by saying, 'It's not those of you who *say*, 'You are my Lord' but those who *show* it. Those are the ones who will come into my home in heaven. And also, it's not for you Do-ers who only want to brag about all the good things that you've succeeded in doing and like to see recorded on your CVs. Heaven's door is open exclusively to those who have walked together with me along life's road in a partnership of love and obedience.'

Peter had to learn this lesson of real love: real love that covers a multitude of faults and failings; real love that doesn't short change others, or in any way give back according to the measure that we feel that they may deserve; real love that forgives and restores the fallen. Rising up out of the sort of forgiveness that Jesus gave him, Peter was to discover the wonderful way that Jesus was still ready to put his faith in him even after his spiritual collapse. This was to leave indelibly written in his heart a practical example of the sort of love and restoration that Jesus gives to failures.

No wonder later on Peter wrote these words:

'The God of all divine undeserved and unending love, who has called you to share in his glory and splendour, after you have gone through a bit of suffering and refining, he will restore you and renew you and make you really strong.'

'Reflect his sympathetic love from your heart with a patient understanding of one another's weaknesses. Show mercy, like him, and don't fall into the trap of pride.'

'Don't give back bad things when that is what you are given. Let your words be a blessing and not a curse, even if that's what happens to you. By doing this you will gain God's blessing.'

'Those who would enjoy a good and happy life keep a watch on your lips so that you don't say anything bad or untruthful. Because the Lord has his eye on you.'

Peter was talking about reflection and relationship. From what he learned and taught we see that in actual fact it's not what we do or don't do off our own bat that ultimately matters with the Lord. What really matters, what is of overriding importance to him, is our relationship with him. So we can be honest about whatever is going on, whether we are up or down, how we are feeling – good or bad – and what we have done or not done, all about our successes or failures. When everything goes pear-shaped we can rant and rave, we can weep and cry, we can believe or doubt, question or complain, we can tell God how confused we are and that we don't know what he is up to. We can even tell him that he has let us down and failed us, but in the end 'relationship' means that we hang on in there when everything, inside us and outside, screams at us to let go.

My, what faith Job had! When everything in his life literally crashed down round his ears and all he could do was throw himself onto the town rubbish tip in despair like a sack of refuse, out of the depths of his pain and confusion, he still cried out, 'Though God kills me, I can't do anything else but go on trusting him.'

That's a bit like Peter talked. When a number of the disciples of Jesus were giving up and Jesus asked those who were left, 'And what about you? Are you off as well?' Peter's reply was a bit strange but very real, 'We're with you, Jesus, because we've nowhere else that we can go. You've got the secret to life now and for eternity. So we are sticking with you.'

Funnily enough Jesus used a similar sort of word when he spoke about the stickability of the marriage relationship. 'Those whom God hath *joined together*. . . don't let people try to separate.' In other words, those who God has brought together are glued together. 'They're stuck – so they stay.'

In Albania most couples are married through the choice of the parents (and generally after that with the couples' agreement), and it seems to work. Why? How? Many years ago in a TV documentary comparing Eastern and Western traditions, a man from the Indian sub-continent commented, 'You marry the one you love, we love the one we marry.'

Relationships grow as people work at them.

* * *

Finally, the way to break free from the power of the failure chain and end up in God's safety net of love is found in the final scene of that early morning beach barbeque.

As Jesus was finishing off those rather embarrassing and unsettling questions that he had been asking him, Peter's chum, John – who was always a bit of a challenge or embarrassment to Peter – wandered across the beach to join them. Peter suddenly saw a way out of this rather personal confrontation and quickly asked Jesus this final question on Galilee Beach, 'But Jesus, what about *him*?'

We are so adept at deflecting attention from the real issues. Just think about the woman by 'Sychar Well' who wanted to talk 'church' when Jesus wanted to talk about cleaning up her act.

'So, what about him?' Peter retorted.

Jesus put Peter firmly in his place by saying, 'What's that got to do with you? You get on following me and don't worry about other people.'

That is perhaps the most challenging but liberating thing for those of us who fail.

It's not what others do or think that matters.

The way out of failure is *to not compare ourselves with others*.

Whoever said, 'Comparisons are odious' knew a thing or two about this problem. One of our biggest failures is not what we do or don't do but looking at others. That is one sure way of really coming unstuck. God made us to be ourselves, not bland or blind copies of others. God is not interested in mass-produced Christians but originals.

It was fascinating at my old Bible College, many years ago now, when we had our preaching classes. We all had to preach a sermon to the class and then everyone had to analyse the other's sermons and methods. As you listened you could often recognise who the student's preaching heroes were. It was the heyday of Dr Martyn Lloyd Jones, and there were those who would emulate his style to become little MLJs. Billy Graham also came over to the UK for a Crusade at that time. Suddenly out the blue you would hear a student or two developing a slight American accent as some of them preached. We waited expectantly for someone one day to conclude his message with a drawling invitation, 'Ah want yeh ter gid up out o' yer seats. . .' Wisely the Principal, after one bad case of 'imitation-itis', said, 'God made Billy Graham and Martin Lloyd Jones to be themselves. You be what God intends you to be.'

So often the reality is that most of our 'failures' are no more than failures to be what others are or expect us to be, or more subtly what we *think* they expect us to be. The only footsteps we have to walk in are those that are Jesus sized. We need to get our eyes off other people and be sure of what the Lord wants us to be. We need to stop thinking about what others do or don't do, say or don't say.

So many people are tied up in knots, almost physically 'bound', by what others have put on them as children or as young people. And not just when we are young! How exciting life becomes when we discover the liberating delight of being free in Jesus! And that's actually what Jesus said was his plan for his followers, 'If the Son of God makes you free, then you *really can* be free.' Failure so many times seems to be measured on those old fashioned sort of scales that use different weights. It's calculated with the heavy weights of all the expectations of those around us whom we are pressurised into wanting to impress. But in the end the only one that really matters is Jesus.

When I stand in front of the Lord Jesus after death I won't be accompanied by my own crowd of cheer leaders, or, thank God, by any of the mob of my accusers. Jesus will say to me, as to Peter, 'Let's go and have a quiet chat somewhere, alone, together.' And then he will ask me what I did about the things *he* told me to do, not what all the rest said were important.

At that point, when it's just me alone with Jesus, most of the things that bother me now won't matter a fig then. All those things that I did to impress people or get their approval won't be worth a thing. And all those things that I thought I had mucked up, and for which I asked forgiveness, I will find the Lord has wonderfully woven into the pattern of my life, and even into his plans for me, to make an amazingly beautiful picture that will cause me to stand back and say, 'Wow! Jesus did we really do all that together? Is that what you made of what I thought was a right pig's ear of my life?' How many of those urgent and demanding things that I thought at the time were so important really won't matter on that day. How many failings, that he has forgiven, will have been changed into glorious evidences of the Lord's ability to transform and use 'all things' for his praise and glory. And the flip side is that some of my most notable 'successes' will probably turn out to be just about as lasting as a pavement artist's beautiful picture after a storm has passed by!

'Don't think about other people,' says Jesus. 'It's just you and me that really matters.'

In this falling apart world I need to constantly remember that God has always had a special place in his heart for 'failures' and has the knack of turning human botch-ups into his opportunities to do a miracle of love for me and others.

The disciples thought it a catastrophe when Lazarus was fatally sick and all Jesus did was to hang around until things got worse and then Lazarus eventually died!

But Jesus said, 'This sickness is not about death, it's something that I'm going to turn around for the glory of God.' He then went to the place of failed hopes and expectations and there at the grave of his friend, with sympathetic tears of love in his eyes, he did something far greater than a healing. He brought Lazarus back from the dead.

Jesus has the habit of turning things upside down (or upside down things right side up), especially failures. 'Just watch me,' he says, 'and see what I can do when there seems no way out.'

That simple yet vital phrase, 'Follow me,' means that we need to keep our eyes constantly on Jesus and not to keep looking over our shoulder at other people. This is the only safety net that 'failures' need – the undeserved love of God in Jesus, not the approval of people. This is what it all basically boils down to. 'Successes' don't appreciate mercy because they don't need it – or so they think! It's those of us who know how weak we are, we are the ones who again and again have to fall, fall, and keep on falling, back into the strong arms of love that catch us every time. We are the ones who have the privilege of hearing our heavenly friend say with his lovely smile, 'Hello. What you again?'

Epilogue

The bottom line to this issue of failure and success is summed up in something that Moses, just before he died, said to the children of Israel, who stumbled and failed so often. After years of experiencing his own personal ups and downs, as well as God-given times of success, Moses told God's people this – and it is recorded in Deuteronomy chapter 33, verses 26 and 27:

> There is no one like the Lord your God.
> You are the people he loves and makes to stand secure and tall.
> He rides all the way across the heavens just so as he can help you;
> He comes as the King of glory in majestic power on the clouds.
>
> This eternal, unchanging, everlasting God is your security and he puts underneath you, like a net, his unfailing and unending arms of love.

This is the only truly dependable safety net that we, who fail, can fall into and be totally secure.